# Listening to The Rhino
## Violence and Healing in a Scientific Age

# Listening to The Rhino

## Violence and Healing in a Scientific Age

JANET O. DALLETT

*With Contributions by*
Pat Britt and The Rhino

An Aequitas Book from
Pleasure Boat Studio: A Literary Press
New York

Part of the royalties from the sale of this book will go to:
    International Rhino Foundation
    IRF White Oak Conservation Center
    581706 White Oak Road
    Yulee, FL 32097

Text design by Susan Ramundo
Cover design by Laura Tolkow
Cover photo by David Mathieson
Printed in the USA

Library of Congress Cataloging-in-Publication Data
    Dallett, Janet.
    Listening to the rhino : violence and healing in a scientific age /
Janet O. Dallett ; with contributions by Pat Britt and the rhino.
        p.    cm.
    Includes bibliographical references.
    ISBN 978-1-929355-45-7
    1. Jungian psychology.   2. Violence—Psychological aspects.
3. Healing.   4. Psychology and religion.   I. Title.

BF175.D325    2008
150.19'54—dc22                                    2008015228

Aequitas Books is an imprint of Pleasure Boat Studio: A Literary Press. This imprint is designed for non-fiction books with a sociological or philosophical theme. Aequitas Books are available through the following:
**SPD (Small Press Distribution)** Tel. 800-869-7553, Fax 510-524-0852
**Partners/West** Tel. 425-227-8486, Fax 425-204-2448
**Baker & Taylor** Tel. 800-775-1100, Fax 800-775-7480
**Ingram** Tel. 615-793-5000, Fax 615-287-5429
**Amazon.com** and **bn.com**

and through
**PLEASURE BOAT STUDIO: A LITERARY PRESS**
*www.pleasureboatstudio.com*
201 West 89th St., Ste. 6F
New York, NY 10024

Contact **Jack Estes**
Tel/Fax: 888-810-5308
Email: *pleasboat@nyc.rr.com*

The rhinoceros goes back to the age of the dinosaur and pterodactyl, and many hunters regard him as one of the most dangerous animals, one of the ugliest and most removed from any vestiges of animal reason. Yet, as I stood and looked at him, I saw through all that was considered inelegant and ugly in his appearance. I saw a strange first essay on the part of creation in the pattern of animal beauty, and the impact of this breakthrough in prehistoric aesthetics was so overwhelming that it was as if I had never encountered anything more dazzling on earth.... Suddenly it was as if not only the gap of time between him and me had been closed, but that a powerful feeling of emancipation was illuminating my war-darkened and industrialized senses.

—Laurens van der Post[1]


It is impossible to go directly on from our cultural state of today if we do not receive increments of strength from our primitive roots.... We must dig down to the primitive, and only from the conflict between civilized man and the barbarian will there come what we need: a new experience of God.

—C. G. Jung[2]

# CONTENTS

# PREFACE

In 1968, as a first-year doctoral student at UCLA, I took a class in the history and systems of psychology. I looked forward to the part about Jung, and was astonished when we finally got there and the professor covered the subject in one sentence: "The Jungians were an esoteric cult that died out many years ago." I knew otherwise. Seven years after Jung's death, interest in his work was already flourishing throughout Europe and North America. The demand for Jungian analytic training programs and clinics was substantial and growing. I myself belonged to a thriving community of Los Angeles Jungian analysts, trainees, and lay people, started during the second world war by several Jewish analysts who escaped from Nazi Germany and began life anew in Southern California. Now the local Jungian population was at least as large as UCLA's psychology department, but my professor was sincere in his belief that Jung's work had all but disappeared. For me, his remark was like the blow of a Zen master driving an essential point home. It focused my attention on the gulf between the two worlds in which I lived—the Jungian on one side, and the cultural and academic mainstream on the other. I was appalled to realize how little each knew or valued of the other. Like the child of divorced parents, I loved them both and longed for them to reconcile. They remain largely estranged, even today, but the hope of bringing them together continues to animate my writing.

Jung was an introvert who devoted his life to making sense of the inner world of dreams, fantasies, and fairy tales; myths, psychotic delusions, and mystic visions; meaningful coincidences; even alchemy. The extraverted values of our culture regard such phenomena as dangerously fascinating, unacceptably peculiar, and as threatening as nuclear war or a deadly virus, exactly the same feelings that introverts have about such socially acceptable extraverted ventures as large cocktail parties and political rallies.

Extraverts tend to see introverts as antisocial and pathologically peculiar. Introverts condemn extraverts as insensitive and lacking in depth. Fortunately for all of us, no one is entirely one way, but most people are more comfortable in one direction and awkward in the other. Extreme one-sidedness is problematical for both.

As Jung defined it, extraversion is the flow of interest and attention toward the outside world, while introversion is interest and attention turned inward. The extravert orients himself by people or objects in the outside world, the introvert by inner factors. In our extraverted culture, most psychotherapists strive to adapt their patients to the demands of society. My introversion biases me toward helping people adapt first to the complexities of their own individual nature, for only then can they make their most valuable contributions to the world.

Introversion notwithstanding, I completed my graduate work with interest, even gusto. Instead of studying clinical psychology, the usual area for psychologists who intend to become therapists, I chose the broader field of experimental psychology. That is, I grounded myself in science: the experimental method, statistical procedures, and the careful, objective observation of measurable facts. Later, at the Jung Institute, I learned to look just as objectively at an inner world that is not so easy to quantify, especially the hidden contents of a mythic location that Jungians call the unconscious. The ensuing years of work with patients have taught me the essentially paradoxical nature of the psyche. Trying to observe both inner and outer happenings without prejudice, not dismissing improbable information just because I do not understand it, I have learned the value of both the linear voices of science and reason and the irrational parts of people expressed in intuition, emotion, the religious impulse, and the drive to create and enjoy art. Both sides must be given their due, for as the following chapters suggest, one-sidedness is the greatest enemy of psychological well-being and perhaps even of physical health.

Our extraverted culture has only rudimentary knowledge of the place where body and psyche meet. However, there were people long ago who sensed that there were links between mind and matter, and some of these people wrote about them over many centuries and in many lands, from Europe to the Far East. They spoke a dream-like, poetic, image-laden, symbolic language typical of all attempts to express what is only partly conscious. The men and women I am talking about were the ancient alchemists, the ones who thought they could turn base matter into gold.

Seen literally, the claims of alchemy are absurd, but Jung discovered that alchemy is a mythic system, which means that it is packed with psychological information in encoded form. Bizarre recipes for turning feces and vomitus into the philosopher's stone or lead into gold make sense when understood as metaphors for redeeming the highest values in human life. Translated into psychological language, the alchemical cooking process sounds a lot like Jungian analysis, and alchemical imagery holds the key to many a modern dream.

This tool and others make it possible to build a living relationship between the beliefs and attitudes of consciousness and the vast inner world. It is a risky venture into the unknown, but when it succeeds, the psyche's self-healing mechanisms are mobilized and a life that has been stuck begins to move, often in remarkable ways. With persistence, the hoped-for outcome is a unique, authentic, meaningful, individual life, alchemical gold indeed in the face of today's enormous pressures to be like everyone else.

I am indebted to friends, colleagues, patients, and, above all, an imaginary rhinoceros for their part in the long, slow process that has refined my understanding of this material. The Rhino horned into my life and my psyche more than three decades ago, planting seeds that lay dormant until 2001. Then James Hollis and the Houston Jung Center invited me to speak at their conference titled "Angels, Demons, Images of the Spirit," and I began to write about the quixotic creature from the world of dreams who somehow managed to cure his dreamer's damaged heart. From there it was a short step to the idea that the ancient alchemical image of freeing the spirit from matter is a precise metaphor for what happens when physical sickness is healed.

A rhinoceros is not exactly a sweet, gentle New Age healer type of creature, though, and the following year Eugene Monick sparked my interest in The Rhino's dangerous other side when he asked me to discuss the problem of violence with a group of Jungian analysts in Scranton, Pennsylvania.

Input from participants in the Houston and Scranton conferences helped refine my thinking about the material presented there. So did questions and comments from audience members in Austin, Denver, Fort Lauderdale, Ithaca, Montreal, Norfolk, Santa Fe, Seattle, Philadelphia, Pittsburgh, and Port Townsend. Meanwhile, a number of individuals read chapters in embryo and gave me the benefit of their thoughtful responses, especially Deborah Wesley, Vance Sherman, Pamela Power, and members of my writers' group including Alex Fowler, Maggie Jamison, Carolyn Latteier, David Mathieson, Margaret McGee, and David Schroeder.

Those of my patients who have allowed me to write about their struggles deserve a special vote of thanks. To protect confidentiality I have changed the names and other identifying information of the ones who want to remain anonymous, while holding to the truth of the inner events that are the focus of my work. I do not want to expose individuals, but to make psychological reality visible, for until the hidden corners of the human psyche can be seen in the context of real lives, such words as "ego," "Self," "archetype," and "shadow" are too abstract to be meaningful.

I am equally grateful to the hundreds of patients who have never found their way into my writing. They have contributed as much to my understanding as the others, even though they remain in the background.

Finally, I thank the man who shares my life. My knowledge of the psyche owes far more than meets the eye to what happens when two stubborn, independent, creative individuals bump together like rocks in a tumbler. David Mathieson's presence as well as his penetrating insights have enabled me to pursue the ideas in this book as far as I possibly could and then, when the time was right, to stop.

# CHAPTER ONE

# Freeing the Spirit Trapped in Sickness

"The world of alchemical symbols definitely does not belong to the rubbish heap of the past, but stands in a very real and living relationship to our most recent discoveries concerning the psychology of the unconscious. Not only does this modern psychological discipline give us the key to the secrets of alchemy, but, conversely, alchemy provides the psychology of the unconscious with a meaningful historical basis."

—C. G. JUNG[3]

Port Townsend, Washington, the town where I live, is noted for its winds. The native people used to say that the spirits stayed in the underworld during the summer, but came back with the winter winds. Then people would go into their longhouses to propitiate the gods with ceremonial dances. Today, locals pay wry homage to the same violent gods when they say that a ritual power outage is required every winter. Fallen trees regularly demolish roofs and block roads, heavy winds interrupt ferry schedules, and every few decades, a bridge blows away.

Port Townsend is also known as a place of healing. Three hundred years ago, the native people sent their sick to a place called Kah-tai to be healed. This is where Port Townsend was built, and today the town's 8400 people manage to support an astonishing number of health professionals—thirty or forty counselors, as many massage therapists, seven physical therapists, and a Jungian analyst. Among thirty-some physicians are three or more who practice alternative forms of medicine. There is also an impressive assortment of New-Age mystics—astrologers, Tarot readers, psychics, dowsers, channelers, spiritual healers of every stripe, and a woman who markets herbal remedies learned from her Gypsy grandmother.

Is there a relationship between the big winds that buffet my home town and its reputation as a locus of healing? In the world of physical reality, I doubt it. I do not imagine that wind heals people, or that healing energies create wind, or even that a third factor causes both healing and wind. In the inner world, however, where symbolic reality and synchronicity prevail, wind and healing do seem to be linked. The thing that connects them is spirit.

The primitive part of the psyche where both language and dreams originate makes no distinction between wind, breath, and spirit. The English word "spirit" derives from a Latin root that means "breath," "breath of a god," and "inspiration," while in languages like Greek and Arabic, the words for *spirit* and *wind* are identical.

Popular culture often mistakenly equates the word "spiritual" with "nice." It is true that the spirit can be as gentle as the caress of a warm summer breeze, but it is just as apt to tear into life with the force, urgency, and destructive power of a hurricane or a wheezing, snorting, rhinoceros on a rampage. The Nazi Holocaust was an incarnation of raw, unmediated spirit. So are the outbreaks of adolescent and preadolescent rage that manifest when children of respectable middle- and upper-class families gun down their parents, teachers, and peers. The September 11th terrorist attacks on New York and Washington also exemplify the destruction the spirit can inflict when people are possessed by it, unrestrained by conscience, compassion, or other human values.

In the 1960s, a great wind of the spirit blew away the inhumanly constricting values of the fifties. Long before most of us understood what was happening, Bob Dylan got it right when he sang that "the times they are a changin'," and "the answer is blowin' in the wind."

The raging spirit of the 1960s devastated some lives and swept others clean. For most it was a little of each. I myself lost a husband to drugs. From the perspective of thirty-some years, however, I would not choose to return to the suffocating consciousness of the fifties, even if in doing so I could bring him back. Something had to change, and when necessary changes are not made voluntarily, the spirit forces them upon us.

The spirit enters the world not only through the big winds of collective change, but in individual ways as well. A bitter divorce, an unexpected pregnancy, a psychotic break, a life-threatening illness—all these things can signal the need for fundamental change. How we understand and relate to such happenings is crucial. If we see them as disasters alone, we will scramble to make life look "normal" again as quickly as possible, seeking the comfort of the familiar even when it is harmful to the greater Self within. Jung called the return to old patterns after a psychic storm "the regressive restoration of the persona." It is an effort to save face, to look good instead of moving courageously forward into an unknown future.

If, on the other hand, we recognize that what has stopped us cold is, in some sense, God, we will try to understand the divine intention, to mediate it in humanly bearable ways, to facilitate the clumsy, half-blind groping of the spirit toward incarnation in our individual lives. This is not an easy task. It is a little like trying to pour the power of a hurricane into an ordinary human body. No wonder the spirit, whose intention seems to be to make us whole, sometimes, paradoxically, makes us sick.

Spirit is, as Jung says, "a most perplexingly ambiguous term."[4] It refers to an animating principle that, "on the primitive level, [is] felt as an invisible, breathlike 'presence'"[5] that is the antithesis of matter and marks the difference between life and death. We give the name spirit to whatever is invisible, intangible, and explicitly non-physical that we nevertheless experience as a force to be reckoned with. When we locate spirit outside ourselves, in the cosmos, we may name it God or the devil. Jung, seeing its source as within, called it the collective unconscious or the archetypal psyche.

The words "cure" and "heal" are also complicated. I am going to use them synonymously, in their ordinary, everyday, dictionary meaning of "restoration of health," or "recovery from disease." When I say "heal," I will not necessarily mean psychological wholeness, but only the return of physical health.

Obscure spiritual factors are involved in the healing of physical illness. Why does one person get sick and another remain healthy under conditions that appear to be identical? Why is it that someone we love dies while our worst enemy lives on and on? Even contemporary medicine, slow to recognize the non-physical aspects of sickness and health, has begun to acknowledge that the psyche plays a role under the rubric of stress. Such phenomena as death by voodoo or the placebo effect suggest that a person's health can be strongly affected by whether he believes he will die or get well; and there is growing recognition that faith in the doctor, the wish to recover, and mood are important ingredients in the healing process. That is why, for instance, mood-elevating drugs are commonly prescribed after surgery. Even though *Time Magazine* devotes an occasional issue to ideas about "how your mind can heal your body,"[6] there is still little recognition of the role played by the spiritual level of the psyche, the collective unconscious.

Ancient healing traditions, on the other hand, have long stressed that only God can heal. As I see it, science can identify and refine conditions that are optimal for healing, including surgeries and medications appropriate to specific illnesses, but beyond that, irrational factors of which we understand little are decisive.

A profound healing process is rarely any gentler than the spirit itself. I sometimes suspect that the prevailing treatments for cancer—a disease whose psychological component can be quite conspicuous—are effective because they are so violent. As Laurens van der Post said, "soft-hearted witch doctors don't heal."[7] A practitioner's ability to facilitate healing of body or psyche will be quite limited unless she can help her patients contain and carry the spirit's violence. An example of this is Seth, a man in his mid-fifties. Seth had a dream spelling out the qualities that he needed:

> I'm in a field where underground oil is in danger of exploding. A firefighter, dressed in a large white suit like an astronaut's, reaches into the ground, then pours something back and forth from one hand to another. It looks like molten metal, and I am amazed that he can do this. He is brave and highly trained,

and he wears gloves that allow him to handle the dangerous hot material. Another fireman runs by and, using direct male talk, demands that a guy move over. He has to check an underground hot spot to keep it from exploding. The man moves over. The fireman does the inspection and makes the necessary adjustments.

Seth associated the space-suited firefighter with Aquarius, icon of the new millennium—the water-bearer who pours the liquefied spirit from one vessel to another. It is as if only in this newly emerging time has the archetype become available to handle what is heating up in Seth's unconscious. The job requires tough protective clothing, courage, training, and direct communication. The unvarnished command—"Move over!"—spoken with authority, contrasts with Seth's gentle, unassertive persona. To integrate the hot molten material inside that he is just beginning to glimpse, he will have to learn "direct male talk," even at the cost of not looking quite so nice.

Soon after Seth told me this dream, a synchronistic occurrence underscored it. Jung described what he called synchronicity as the connecting factor between events that the psyche perceives as related, even though there can be no cause-and-effect relationship between them. Meaning, rather than causality, is what links synchronistic events. Through synchronicity, the familiar world of everyday reality is opened to the realm of spirit. It is as if, for a moment, the boundary between different realities dissolves and the uncanny becomes visible. In the metaphor of the ancient alchemists, this is a time when the spirit can descend into matter.

On the occasion in question, my husband and I walk to dinner at our favorite Mexican restaurant. There is no sidewalk, so we travel in the nearly empty parking lane, wearing blinking red reflector lights and waving flashlights to make drivers aware of us. It is a dark, rainy, winter evening and I feel unusually vulnerable in spite of our precautions. Just before we enter the restaurant, we see flashing red and blue lights on the highway ahead. We are seated at a table overlooking a large parking lot where we have a ringside view of what happens next. On the face of it, practical, scientific, and rational considerations dictate the entire drama, but beneath the surface a primitive, non-rational level of the psyche is engaged. It is as if we were in a dream. Before we finish our meal, we will have taken part in a profound healing ritual.

Four fire engines, several police cars, and an aid car have arrived. Our waitress reports that a man trying to cross the highway was hit by a woman driver. "Poor woman," she says. I am startled, then realize that she is right. On a night like this, the driver is as much a victim of circumstance as the man who was hit.

A rumor that the man is decapitated proves not to be true, but he does have severe head injuries and will be airlifted to Seattle for treatment. The aid car moves him from the highway to the parking lot, and firefighters spread over the area. Like the ones in Seth's dream, they wear space-age coveralls, helmets, and boots. Men and women alike employ "direct male talk," instructing drivers to move their vehicles quickly away from the scene.

Then the firemen and women cluster together near the aid car. By now, the complete attention of scores of rescue workers and passersby is focused on the uncertain fate of an unnamed victim. Minutes later we hear the sound of the chopper. As one, the assembled fire people raise torchlike red flares toward the sky, and the giant bird descends into the fiery light like some latter-day incarnation of the holy spirit.

Suddenly, the rotors stop. In the silence it is as if the big bird has died, and when a white-wrapped figure is laid on the ground I am convinced that the victim, too, is dead. The fire people encircle him, shuffling their feet to move closer and closer until their shoulders all touch and the wounded one, dead or alive, is shielded while medics do what they can. Then, miraculously, a stretcher is transferred to the belly of the bird, the blades begin to rotate, and the spirit ascends once more.

Tears suddenly wet my face. "The last guy they airlifted to Seattle didn't make it," I say, hardly daring to hope that this time the outcome will be different. The comatose stranger has co-opted my attention, my energy, my prayers, and I am only one of a chance community of well-wishers bent on his survival. For his part, he is carrying the consequences of human vulnerability for us all. But for the grace of God, he could have been any one of us.

Two weeks later, the Port Townsend *Leader* reports that the injured man, a 60-year-old visitor from San Francisco, is in satisfactory condition. I feel strangely vindicated. The ritual was successful, my energy well spent.

The ancient alchemists believed that the spirit sometimes comes down from the sky like a rescue helicopter and then cannot get off the ground again. They said it is trapped in matter. As they saw it, the work of alchemy could set the spirit free, thereby healing both body and soul. One text put it this way:

"This birth [release of the spirit from matter] conquers the subtle and spiritual sickness in the human mind and also all bodily defects, within as well as without."[8]

An alchemist's drawing of what he saw in his laboratory flask when the spirit was freed from the embrace of physical matter shows a white dove in a tightly stopped spherical vessel. The bird is flying toward the top of the flask, away from a black, malignant-appearing dead animal that is flattened against the bottom. It is as if, within the vessel of the alchemist's psyche, the bird of the spirit has ceased to be trapped in the blackness of exclusively animal existence.

The psychological issues portrayed by this imagery are still alive today and find symbolic expression in contemporary dreams. For instance, a woman artist dreams that birds are confined in a large wooden box and will die unless they are set free. An artist in the dream releases the birds by doing her painting. This suggests that, outside the dream, the dreamer's spirit will die if she stops painting.

In a dream published by Edinger,[9] the dreamer catches a golden-colored fish whose blood he is required to extract and heat. The blood is in constant danger of clotting, and it is essential to keep it fluid. Edinger sees the fish as an image of Christ. I see its blood as akin to the divine essence. Keeping the blood from congealing is similar to keeping the spirit from getting stuck in matter.

A patient once told me that she had long dismissed my references to alchemy as eccentric aberrations, but later she understood that alchemy is "about transforming one thing into something entirely different." In the aftermath of a near-death experience, she realized that the less-than-perfect life about which she had complained for years was actually incomparably valuable. Speaking in the symbolic language of dreams and myth, the alchemists would say that she had finally cooked her feces, vomit, and urine long enough to turn the disgusting brew of her life into gold.

Jung discovered that the chemical reactions that alchemists saw in their vessels served as projection screens for processes deep in the unconscious, specifically those involved in the psyche's transformation. Just as stories about God mirror certain aspects of the archetypal psyche, so alchemical assertions that make no sense in literal reality are symbolic expressions of the mysteries of psychic change. The hard part—as complicated as extracting meaning from dreams—is translating the ancient formulas and recipes into contemporary psychological language. For instance, what does it really mean to say that the spirit descends into matter?

In essence, "spirit caught in matter" is an amalgam of two things that are meant to be separate. It depicts a failure to discriminate between the symbolic (spiritual) and the literal (material) realms. It is a confusion between inner/psychological realities and literal outer-world ones. Both are essential parts of the whole, but problems arise when they are mixed up with each other.

There are many possible applications in our lives. For one, the idea of spirit imprisoned in matter seems related to fundamentalism. The fundamentalist fallacy is to take literally what belongs to the inner, symbolic, or spiritual realm. Thus, for instance, Christian fundamentalism believes that everything in the Bible is true at the most concrete level, even if—like the virgin birth—it is impossible in ordinary reality.

No one is completely free of the fundamentalist psyche. In the United States today, for instance, a common unexamined assumption is that happiness depends on having a lot of possessions or making large amounts of money. We are similarly driven to seek spiritual well-being in material substances such as Prozac, alcohol, or chocolate. Even the Internet is a concrete recipient of fond inner fantasies, a dynamic that becomes problematical when spiritual life is addictively trapped there.

Something akin to fundamentalist fervor grips us whenever we feel compelled to act out a powerful image or emotion instead of either giving it symbolic expression or holding it inwardly. At the beginning of an analytic process, patients frequently feel intense pressure to *do* something—change the world, change others, change themselves—when containment and self-reflection are needed. When the fundamentalist fallacy grows unchecked it frequently culminates in violence—screaming at a spouse, shooting an abortionist, or crashing an airliner into the Twin Towers—driven by the spirit of divine righteousness misdirected into concrete, outer-world reality. Only when our godlike emotions are freed from such literal misunderstandings of God's will can we bear them internally and redirect their expression into humanly viable forms, behavior that does not distort or brutalize the soul.

At another level, the idea of spirit trapped in matter seems to describe the psychological aspect of physical illness. In that case, the work of freeing the spirit from matter may heal the body as well as the soul.

In my experience, all sicknesses and injuries have a psychological component, even those that are not primarily psychosomatic. I do not intend to minimize the role of viruses and bacteria, only to point out that spirit or psyche is *also* involved, something our culture, with its bias toward scientific materialism, tends to overlook.

In some cases, the spirit in a disease can be made conscious and transformed into something intangible such as intense emotional suffering, or a living image, perhaps a work of art or an imaginary friend or enemy—divine, human, or even a talking animal. Then the illness may disappear. It is as if what had been stuck in the body were converted into a non-physical form. That is to say that disease itself is a manifestation of the spirit, and consciousness can sometimes release it from its bondage in protoplasm by allowing it to take a different form.

I first became aware of this phenomenon in the late 1960s, when I began to practice Jungian analysis and noticed that patients who came to a session with the flu or a cold sometimes recovered during the hour. Initially, I assumed that they were momentarily distracted from their symptoms. Over the years, however, quite a few people came back the next week and said, "It's the funniest thing. I was really sick last week, but when we worked on that dream I began to feel better, and by the time I got home my temperature was normal. The flu just disappeared."

This does not happen every day, but it has occurred often enough to get my attention, and sometimes the illness is more serious than a cold. One patient recovered from an attack of functional blindness when she began to paint the images in her inner vision. Others have been mysteriously cured of such sicknesses as cancer, heart disease, and arthritis as an apparent side effect of analysis.

Note that I said side effect. Intentionally trying to cure sickness with analysis rarely works, but careful attention to the psyche for its own sake affects the body in surprising ways.

At the level of literal, scientific reality, I have no idea of the mechanism for this kind of healing; but I know it does happen and I find the alchemical metaphor a fruitful way to think about it. In the 1970s, I experienced something of the sort myself when I took part in a charismatic prayer group. One evening I went to a meeting of the group with a bad case of flu, and asked for prayers for healing. Several people formed a circle and put their hands on me, all the while praying in a cacophony of tongues and ordinary

English. I felt a jolt, as if an electrical charge had passed through my body. My head cleared and all the symptoms vanished. While I was driving home I began to weep. For the first time, I allowed myself to feel the full impact of my grief for a beloved mentor who had recently been disabled by a stroke. By the time I got home my temperature was normal. The symptoms did not recur.

With hindsight, this is how I see what happened: When I first heard of my mentor's stroke, I was struck as if by lightning. The shock was more than my psyche could bear, and my body took the overload. Somehow, the prayer caused me to re-experience the shock, permitting the spirit to soften into the grief that I was now ready to tolerate.

I do not subscribe to the view, common in New Age circles, that if you get sick you are doing something wrong. Carried to its logical conclusion, that implies that if you did everything right, your body would live forever. As I see it, the spirit expresses itself in many ways in the individual life, some that we see as good, others as bad. Sickness is a manifestation of spirit that we think of as bad, and a person who is strong enough and conscious enough can sometimes find a less concrete and physical way to carry the same material. What happens then, when illness irrationally leaves the body, often looks like a miracle.

Seth, the man who dreamed about the Aquarian firefighters, was raised by a paranoid schizophrenic father and a mother who idealized his younger brother while projecting evil on Seth. By rights, Seth should have gone crazy. I attribute the fact that he did not to the intense and meaningful connection he made to the Catholic church. He paid a high price, however, for the Church taught him to deal with his intolerable life by repressing his emotions, especially the anger, a healthy reaction to abuse.

After Seth grew up, an enormous effort of will, several kinds of therapy, and various spiritual practices enabled him to hold a demanding job for thirty-six years, but his emotions were virtually anesthetized. He was chronically depressed and developed the fatigue and painful muscles and joints of fibromyalgia. In his late fifties, he dreamed that an unknown woman therapist told him:

"We can make progress, but to be well requires rage; that is, it is necessary to be free to release the long stored anger. You must get mad."

Soon after this, Seth retired from his job, moved to Port Townsend, and began analysis. As the hot material in his unconscious began to surface, he had dream after dream of impending disaster—flood, fire, earthquake, and tornado. Meanwhile, he stopped taking antidepressants and felt an upsurge of energy. With massage in addition to analysis, the stiffness and pain in his body began to disappear, and emotional color gradually entered his life. I imagine that the space-suited firefighter within him—the one who knows how to do the job safely—has avoided a disastrous explosion by releasing the spirit imprisoned in Seth's body bit by bit, a little at a time.

This slow and careful pace reflects the wisdom of the psyche so disregarded today, a path directed from within. We live in an artificial and speeded-up world that demands quick fixes and freedom from pain. However, when a person can learn to love his symptoms, irrational as this may seem, and try to understand and honor the messages they bring, sickness is transformed into a guide that leads, in its leisurely, rambling way, to the greatest treasure to be found: an authentic, conscious, and meaningful individual life.

# CHAPTER TWO

# The Rhino[10]

[In fairy tales], anyone who earns the gratitude of animals, or whom they help for any reason, invariably wins out. This is . . . psychologically of the utmost importance, because it means that in the conflict between good and evil the decisive factor is . . . the animal soul; anyone who has it with him is victorious. . . . [This] is subject only to one condition: that the hero keep faith with the animal.

—MARIE-LOUISE VON FRANZ[11]

Pat Britt was scheduled to die of a damaged heart more than thirty years ago, but she surprised everyone. Today, in her eighth decade, her life is more vital and productive than that of most people half her age. The spirit released from her illness took the form of a large, gravelly voiced rhinoceros. He calls himself The Rhino, and he has frequented her dreams and fantasies since the 1970s. Pat says The Rhino came into her life because she was "hung up on science." As she puts it, "I had a left-brain approach to everything, and that had to change."

Pat and The Rhino are my co-authors and I am using her real name. She is one of the most private people I know, but The Rhino is the opposite, and after consulting him she decided to sacrifice her anonymity and lay public claim to her story.

On December 7, 1941, the day the Japanese attacked Pearl Harbor, an acute strep infection attacked Pat's body. She was ten years old and had scarlet fever. In the next decade she had rheumatic fever three times, and she experienced three more episodes between the ages of twenty and forty.

When she was forty-one, she came down with sub-acute bacterial endocarditis. An echocardiogram showed that the aortic and mitral valves of her heart were severely scarred, and she was told she was going to die. Her kidneys were failing and her system was so flooded with toxins that she felt as if she had cotton wool in her head. She begged for dialysis, knowing that it would clear her head, but it was rationed then, and it was refused because her case was considered too hopeless to merit "wasting" the costly and scarce procedure. She was also denied a valve replacement because, said the doctor, she was too sick to survive the surgery. Later, after The Rhino came into her life, Pat became so insistent that she was finally allowed dialysis every six weeks, gradually increasing up to twice a week. The procedure relieved her symptoms but could not repair her damaged heart.

I first met Pat when she came to my office in July of 1974. I was 41 years old, and was just finishing my training at the C. G. Jung Institute in Los Angeles. Pat was 43 and was so sick that her face was blue. Lee Meyerhoff, her former therapist, had referred her to me because, she recently informed me wryly, he could not convince her to face her imminent death and believed that I might be able to.

Lee had a friend named Julia who was dying of inoperable, metastasized lung cancer and was in analysis with me. Her medical picture was hopeless, and the first dream she brought to analysis confirmed the poor prognosis:

> I am on stage, rehearsing for an opera in which I am to sing a lead role. I am eating a purple popsicle, and refuse to take it out of my mouth. The stage manager fires me for my arrogant attitude, and I don't care.

The initial dream in analysis typically assesses the dreamer's psychological situation and often predicts the outcome with uncanny accuracy. Julia's dream recognized that she had a specific, individual combination of talents to contribute to the world. That is, she had a destiny—a leading role in the opera of life. However, she childishly refused to cooperate. As a result the stage manager was going to kick her out of life, and she did not care. I see the stage manager as a God-image, or what Jung called the Self: the archetypal center of the total psyche that we experience as if it were God.

When someone has an archetypal fate, she can cooperate with it or not. However, refusing to take the assigned role changes nothing but the way it manifests, which is apt to be more negative if denied. This is the fallacy in the popular notion that you can do whatever you want in life, something that is true only if what you want is congruent with the kind of person you are. The Self behaves as if it were a sort of spiritual DNA that preprograms certain aspects of a person. An acorn cannot become a walnut tree, no matter how hard it tries. However, if we get connected to our program, and pay careful attention to it, then we can often do what we want even in the face of unfriendly outer circumstances, for something beyond the ego comes to our aid. Then it is even easy. This is an aspect of what The Rhino means when he says to Pat, as he often does in her dreams, "If it's worth doing, it's worth doing easily!"

Julia died a year and a half later. No thanks to me, she rushed to meet death with open arms. Pat, on the other hand, appeared to be in denial, but her initial dream hinted that she was actually in touch with the reality of a destiny quite different from Julia's:

> In the first part of the dream, Pat is invited to adopt a newborn pastel pink caracal kitten. She doesn't want it, but no one else does either, and she takes pity on it. Then she goes for a walk. In her words:
>
> I am walking down a trail covered in redwood bark. There are snakes all over, some beside the path and some coming up through the redwood dust against my bare feet. The mood of the place is enchantment. The snakes are real and solid, but the landscape is an impressionistic painting. I know I have discovered an incredible treasure. Some of the larger snakes are pythons, and there is one large, dark, mottled snake that I can't identify. He is trying to be friendly and keeps wrapping himself around my ankle. I want to enjoy him, but I am afraid he might be poisonous, so think it would be foolish to pick him up. Finally, I see his head and realize he is a whip snake. I drape him over my shoulder and walk on.
>
> A small rhinoceros threatens to charge me. He keeps hesitating, but finally makes the charge. I step aside and, as he passes, I catch him by the horn and hold him. Then he turns into a unicorn. The three of us—snake, unicorn, and I—walk on down the trail together.

Here, at the onset of analysis, Pat accepts the values of an inner world that science largely dismisses. She embraces the culturally rejected psyche three times: first in the form of an unnaturally colored wildcat baby, then as a potentially dangerous snake—perhaps an allusion to Satan himself, who tempts people to eat the dangerous fruit of consciousness; and finally, like the Old-Testament Jacob, who wrestled with the dark angel of God and would not let go until his adversary blessed him, she faces and takes hold of her deadly opponent. As soon as she grasps the monster by its horn, The Rhino becomes a benevolent companion. This foreshadows what would happen in her analysis, in the course of which, against all odds, her illness was transformed into a steadfast inner partner.

As if to underscore the positive prognosis, six weeks later Pat dreamed, "A piece of lead turns to gold." At the time her only knowledge of alchemy was the popular picture of the slightly mad scientist who imagines that he can literally turn base metal into gold. However, her unconscious picked this image to express the inner changes under way, in which the leaden burden of severe physical illness was becoming a spiritual process of the highest value and meaning.

The Rhino has been the central figure in hundreds of Pat's dreams, continuing still today. On the one hand, he is a nearly human companion, with his own sometimes-whimsical desires. On the other, he is like a divine being—a capricious and unpredictable God-image offering profound spiritual wisdom to anyone with the ears to hear it.

Unicorns and unicorn-like animals appear in mythic traditions throughout the world, where divine and demonic qualities are attributed to them. Jung writes,

> In Christian picture-language the unicorn . . . is a symbol of
> the spermatic Word or Spirit[12]; and The two gigantic beings,
> Og and the unicorn, are reminiscent of Behemoth and
> Leviathan, the two manifestations of Jehovah. . . . personifica-
> tions of the daemonic forces of nature. The power of God re-
> veals itself not only in the spirit of man, but in the fierce
> animality of nature both in man and outside him.[13]

The unicorn is said to be Christ, the Holy Spirit, and even Mercurius, the two-faced, good-and-evil figure that in alchemy symbol-
izes the principle of transformation. Despite the phallic appearance
of its single horn, this mythic animal is seen as both masculine and
feminine, penetrating and passively receptive. It is also paradoxically
good and evil, tough as a judge and gentle as a savior.

Throughout the world, animals with a central horn have long
been believed to bring healing. Some cultures ascribe magical qualities specifically to the horn, said to bestow strength, health, masculine sexual prowess, and fertility. In the Middle and Far East, cups
made of rhinoceros horn are still sold today to protect their owners
from being poisoned. Such beliefs have made an endangered species
of rhinoceroses, killed for the high price their horns will bring.

In outer reality, Pat is involved in efforts to save the rhinoceros from extinction. In the inner world, some of her dreams emphasize the power of the unicorn's or The Rhino's horn. One such
dream takes place at a watering-hole in East Africa that Pat, who
has traveled all over the world, had previously visited in real life:

> I am watching the water bubble out of the ground at Mzima
> Springs. The sky is rosy-gray, dawn-softened. A herd of ze-
> bras drifts by, silken, shifting stripes against velvet hills, creat-

ing an impressionistic water color. I have a sense of being semi-fluid, of flowing with the zebras, the wind and the water.

I want to discover the secret of the place, so I go to the source of the spring, where a group of rhinos are clustered. Just as the sun comes up, a unicorn appears. He thrusts his horn into the spring, remaining motionless for several minutes. Finally he straightens up and says, 'I am the secret of the spring. It must be renewed by a unicorn every morning at dawn.'

Then, by degrees, the unicorn becomes a rhino again and moves off with the herd.

This dream, which Pat had during the first year of her analysis, shows how ambiguous The Rhino's status is. Does he belong to the world of outer reality or only to the inner? He moves back and forth between being an ordinary rhinoceros at a real location that Pat has visited and a mythical beast at a magical spring.

It is not necessary to choose between these different aspects of his identity. The black and white zebra stripes are a reminder that opposite qualities can co-exist in a single animal, and in fact The Rhino brings many opposites together. His paradoxical messages range from the sublime to the ridiculous, from grand philosophical observations to gratuitous mockery and just plain nonsense. The part of the psyche he embodies manifests simultaneously as a life-threatening illness and a benevolent inner figure.

This dream and others engage Pat in what Jung saw as the central spiritual task of our time, coming to terms with the problem of opposites. In the psyche, factors that appear to be mutually contradictory actually co-exist. If we look deeply enough we discover that we are good *and* evil, male *and* female, conscious *and* unconscious. When we lose sight of this we tend to split the world, claiming good for ourselves and projecting evil on others. The capacity to tolerate paradox, holding the opposites together inside, is consequently of the utmost practical importance.

Jung says, "Without the experience of the opposites there is no experience of wholeness and hence no inner approach to the sacred figures."[14] However, tolerating paradox can be excruciating. "The view that good and evil are spiritual forces outside us, and that man is caught in the conflict between them, is more bearable by far than the insight that the opposites are the ineradicable and indispensable preconditions of all psychic life, so much so that life itself is guilt."[15]

As a young analyst, I did not understand the importance of The Rhino's paradoxical nature, and kept trying to formulate his meaning unambiguously. Every time I made what I thought was an erudite synopsis of him—healer, God-image, Self, guide to the soul, animus, or whatever—he responded with a dream that proved me wrong. He seemed to be mocking my earnest efforts, but it was not in my heart to resent him, for as far as I could tell, he was saving Pat's life. Inexplicably, her health grew steadily better. The need for dialysis diminished and eventually came to an end. Belatedly, her doctor wanted to do a valve replacement, but she turned it down because, she said, she was too well. All things considered, I was not about to try to convince her to face her death. Instead, I suggested that she honor The Rhino by making images of his many transformations. She painted his picture, carved him in wood, had him cast in bronze, and would occasionally allude to him in a poem. In 1990, before evidence came to light that Mt. Kilimanjaro's glaciers were melting, she wrote:

## Sonnet to Kilimanjaro

You stand alone, unchallenged on the plain,
and hide your head from common prying eyes.
Remote, majestic, set in gold you reign,
all wrapt in velvet grass and jeweled skies.

You thrust your sacred horn up through the cloud,
to rend the sky, to pierce the orange moon.
You tuck your rocky feet beneath a shroud
of grass and thorn to hide your fiery womb.

You will endure when earth is laid to waste,
when all we love is lost in endless night.
May I invade your secret slopes in haste,
to reach your snowy head in fading light?

May I caress your scaly dragon skin,
and touch the rhino heart that lies within?

Pat reports that the mountain's answer to her request was **no**:
Later that year she undertook to fulfill a lifelong wish to climb
Kilimanjaro, but she says she "only" made it to 13,000 feet. Not
bad for someone presumed to be fatally ill!

I have often wondered why Pat was so vulnerable to sickness
as a child. On the reductive level that looks to early childhood experience for the cause of problems, I can find nothing. She was
not neglected or abused. The only major trauma was illness itself.
The explanation that satisfies me belongs to the prospective, tele-
ological level concerned with purpose or meaning. At a watershed

moment in American history when World War II began, the psychic atmosphere in this country was disturbed, just as it is today. The undeveloped egos of children are particularly vulnerable to this kind of disturbance. In Jungian language an archetype was *constellated*. Call it the archetype of invasion. Speaking in their strange, symbolic language, the ancient alchemists might have said that the spirit wanted to incarnate and, seeking someone to serve it, it took the form of an illness and descended into the body of an intelligent, sensitive, self-reflective young child who was exceptionally open to it. Unfortunately, it got stuck there and waited many years to be released. Unlikely as such a scenario seems in mundane reality, the Rhino dreams hint that, from the psyche's mythic perspective, something of the sort was going on. In one dream, at a time when Pat was wrestling with the question of why The Rhino came to her, he states clearly that Pat's purpose in life is to serve him:

> I am sitting on a hill, watching the sunset. After the last sparks from the sun disappear over the horizon, a fiery ball gradually rises in the west. I think the sun is reappearing, but soon realize that it is much smaller and closer to me than the sun. It floats in my direction and lands near me, revealing itself to be The Rhino, fiery in the reflected light. He sits next to me, assuming something like a lotus position. I have been wanting to question him, so I say, 'What do you want me to do?'
>
> He says, 'Why, to serve my purposes, of course.'
>
> That doesn't help much, so I ask, 'What are your purposes?' and he replies, 'Don't ask me idle questions. They're your own purposes, so you needn't be so inquisitive. Anyway, it can't be said. But I'll demonstrate, from my own point of view.'

The dream goes on to give a glimpse of the perspective of the unmediated spirit, which can be exasperatingly opaque to rational understanding:

> First Pat finds herself among snow-covered hills, wearing strange short skis on which she and others are playing. She runs first on level ground, then downhill on these skis, and glides uphill on the momentum. Later she experiments with balancing on her hands on the skis and doing backward flips. Eventually she reaches the top of the tallest hill, where she finds a beautiful multicolored balloon. She gets into the basket, starts the burner and takes off, then sees that the balloon is The Rhino, with a basket cable attached to each leg. He has a star impaled on his horn.
>
> The balloon lands in the driveway of Pat's house, which is filled with water, forming a small lake. Pat decides not to ask why they have landed or even to comment.
>
> Next a dolphin nudges her and says it has been assigned to her. The Rhino is wallowing in the lake. Pat walks over to him and asks 'What is the message?'
>
> He says, 'How should I know? I'm just a rhinoceros.'

Henry Miller once said, "Until we accept the fact that life itself is founded in mystery, we shall learn nothing." Out of respect for the mystery, I am going to follow Pat's lead and not ask too many questions about the events in this dream. However, I do want to mention that the star on The Rhino's horn may allude to the Self. Stars are connected with The Rhino in many of the dreams, an ongoing reminder that Pat's destiny is, as it were, written in the stars.

Additional insight into the meaning of the star came in a dream many years later, at a time when Pat was trying to select and arrange some of her dreams in a way that might clarify The Rhino's message. This was not an easy task, and she was having trouble with it.

In the dream, she was building a table made of five sections. Each section was carved of a single piece of wood, and consisted of a leg and a portion of tabletop. Each leg was carved with certain African animals: 1) antelopes; 2) lions and leopards; 3) elephants; 4) a python, zebras, and giraffes; and 5) The Rhino. The top of each section was made of smooth, velvet-grained wood whose pieces had to be fitted together to make the tabletop. Pat said:

The difficulty is that there are five sections. It seems obvious that there should be only four, but no four of them will fit together properly.

I finally give up and go to sit on the hillside. The Rhino is nearby, eating a eucalyptus. He says, 'You need to use all the pieces, but in the right order. Let them decide.'

So I go back to the table. I set up the first piece (the antelopes). When I put the lions next to it they don't join, but the elephants snap into place. The lions fit on the other side. At that point, the last two pieces fit easily. The tabletop is then a circle, with empty space in the center forming a five-pointed star.

Once all the pieces are in place, the opening fills with lapis, its sparkling gold flecks alive with light. Looking at the star opening is like looking through a crack in the world, out into the cosmos.

So we see that The Rhino's message, when properly put together, gives a glimpse through the star into eternity. Viewed under the aspect of eternity, life's problem often look quite different than they do from the limited perspective of human consciousness, a point that all the major religions emphasize. By the same token, illness that cannot be cured by ordinary means is sometimes healed by a relationship to otherworldly powers.

The belief that God can cure sickness is very old. C. A. Meier describes the rite of incubation practiced in ancient Greece, saying that, from near and far "there came to the ... [sanctuary of Asclepius, god of healing] . . . sick people who hoped to be cured—especially if medical skill had proved unavailing or held out no hope."[16] After rituals to cleanse them, supplicants were confined in a cave or hole in the ground within the temple, alone or in the company of snakes. They had to stay there until the god appeared to them in a healing dream or vision. Sometimes the god came in the form of an animal.

Pat's process resembles incubation in several ways: Soon after she turned to the unconscious for help, a superhuman being appeared in her dreams in the form of a ponderous and primitive animal, and she soon began to get well. Moreover, in her initial dream she is surrounded by snakes, and in outer reality she keeps snakes as pets.

However, there is an important difference between incubation and the myth that Pat's psyche has generated. The Greek view, like the Christian one, is that God comes in order to heal

27

people. The Rhino's perspective is not so anthropocentric. We may imagine that he came to save Pat, but he says the opposite: that Pat was born to serve *him*, and that he is her purpose in life.

The Rhino's view is like that of the alchemists who believed that the purpose of their work was to redeem God or the son of God. However, the son to whom they referred was not Christ, but a figure called the son of the philosophers. Jung points out that if the divine son the alchemists imagined had been a true opposite to Christ he would have been female. Instead, he was a hermaphroditic underworld divinity, "a fabulous being conforming to the nature of the primordial mother."[17] Christ's job is to redeem man the microcosm, but the son of the philosophers is here to save the macrocosm—the whole universe.

The son of the philosophers resembles the Venus of Willendorf in some ways, but he has a masculine name and, like The Rhino, "carries in himself the weight of the earth and the whole fabulous nature of primordial animality."[18]

The compensatory relationship that exists between Christ and the alchemical son of the philosophers is mirrored in Pat's dreams: Unlike Christ, who is a bright, daylight image of God, The Rhino, like the son of the philosophers, is an earthy, dark, nighttime divinity. So it is that in some dreams the Rhino comes to earth at the precise moment that the last sparks of sunlight vanish.

Even though Pat must serve The Rhino, he responds to her attentions by helping and supporting her. In 1982, after I decided to leave Los Angeles and move to the Pacific Northwest, he gave Pat the reassuring message that he, at least, would always be there to show her the way. She was in Africa when she had this dream, and The Rhino once again appears at nightfall:

I am walking across the pan in Mabuasehube, looking for The Rhino. I am supposed to meet him at sunset, but the sun is already on the horizon, flattened between earth and sky. I have been walking for over an hour, but my destination, a dead tree on the edge of the pan, looks no closer. A cloud of springbok come pronking from the east, rosy in the glow of the vanishing sun. As they pass, they whisper, 'Run. The darkness is pursuing us.'

A lone gemsbok hurries past. A soft breeze passes over me, and I shiver, knowing that darkness has overtaken me. An owl flies overhead. The pan has become a dusty purple sea, surrounded by black hills. The Great Rhino appears in the sky, his front leg pointing in the direction I am to travel. Now the sky darkens from grey to black and the stars blaze with a cold white fire. I hurry on, afraid I will miss The Rhino.

Finally, I come to the dead tree and find The Rhino waiting under it, silver in the starlight. I am relieved to see him and say, 'I was afraid you would be gone by now.'

He says, 'Don't be stupid. I'm always here in the sky. How else would you find your way?' I look again and realize that he is made of stars.

I suspect that the dead tree alludes to the end of our work, and that The Rhino is reminding Pat that neither his existence nor hers depends on me. Earlier, she had had a number of dreams about a large and miraculous tree which, in retrospect, I believe referred to the analytic function of connecting the realm of ordinary reality with the upper world of the spirit and also the underworld.

The first of these dreams, five years earlier, shows the power and numinosity of the tree when it was alive:

I was standing under a great white tree that held the sun and moon in its branches. Next to me the unicorn was holding a star on the end of his horn. I reached for the star, but as I touched it, it shot off his horn and flew into the top branches of the tree where it was caught and held. It seemed very important that I reach the star, so I pulled myself up into the tree and began to climb it.

The climb was incredibly difficult, partly because the distance from each branch to the next was too great to reach, partly because I had to stay centered between the hot sun and the terribly cold moon, but I finally reached the highest point in the tree and found the star. This time I was reluctant to touch it, afraid it would fly away. I looked down through the tree and the scene was transformed. The tree was covered with leaves and set in a grassy meadow, full of irises. I looked back at the star and it seemed to come toward me. As soon as I touched it, it became a vast planet and I was sitting on it.

I stood up and looked around. In front of me was a great white tree, with the sun and the moon caught in its branches. The Rhino was standing in front of it, with a star caught on his horn. He said, 'That was certainly a lot of trouble to come back to the same old place.'

The circular course of this dream is reminiscent of stories that exist in many spiritual traditions, in which the hero sets out seeking treasure of one sort or another and eventually returns home, only to find what he has been looking for in his own back yard.

The enormous archetypal tree has many parallels in alchemy and other mythologies. In Norse mythology, the great world tree connects heaven, earth, and the underworld. As Pat's analyst, I had carried this mediating role, but after I said I was going to move, she began to find her own relationship to The Rhino. By the time I left she had accepted that she had a genuine responsibility to serve this apparently divine inner figure, and we both felt that her continued good health depended on it. For all practical purposes she was well now, but from a medical standpoint there was nothing to prevent her from getting sick again, as she had done repeatedly before her relationship with The Rhino.

For nine years The Rhino's requirements had been satisfied by our analytic hours, whose exclusive purpose was to discuss the latest Rhino dream, but as my last day in Los Angeles drew near he became more demanding. Pat dreamed the following:

I am at a window in a tall building, looking down at an interchange where four major freeways come together. It is night, and the cars look like pieces of light flowing below me. Around me are dozens of brightly lighted tall buildings, and the stars mirror the rivers of light below. Only the buildings seem fixed. Earth and sky are in constant motion, flowing toward the north.

Below, The Rhino approaches the base of a building. He nudges it with his horn and it begins to move, enters the freeway, and is soon moving north. Other buildings join it. Eventually The Rhino pushes the building I am in. It shakes briefly and joins the stream.

As we flow north, the buildings become trains of glass cubes, then large glass bubbles, not unlike automobiles. Soon we are far from any city and mountains surround us. The only light is from stars and the glowing bubbles on the highway. Abruptly, my bubble turns off the road, proceeds down an unpaved track, and stops under a large tree. There is snow all around.

The Rhino is standing under the tree with a lantern hung on his horn. He says, 'It's about time you got home. I want my dinner.'

I walk into the house, go to the cupboard, shovel a grainy substance into a bowl, add some honey, and give it to The Rhino. He eats it and says, 'Now we can get down to work.' Still carrying the lantern, he leads me outside and we begin to plant starlight in sweeping, irregular rows along the hillside, under the snow.

A month later, in January, 1983, Pat and I ended our work. She and her housemate Gwen took The Rhino's advice and began to look farther north for a place to live. It would be two years before they could move, but The Rhino was raring to go and became increasingly specific about his expectations. In one dream, he walked into a house while Pat and Gwen were moving in, and asked where his room was. Pat told him to pick out whatever he wanted. He was very fussy, but finally settled on a deck with a hot tub and a water view. The view was crucial because, he said, "Rhinos must plan ahead, and the only way to do that is to see what's in front of you." In a dream the following week, he carried Pat and Gwen on his back to a house overlooking Puget Sound.

Near the end of 1984, Pat, Gwen, and Pat's ailing, 86-year-old mother moved to Marrowstone Island near where I was living in Port Townsend. They brought The Rhino and many outer-world pets including two dogs, three cats, four snakes, an iguana, and a desert tortoise, later to be joined by peacocks, songbirds, and turtles. I imagined that the move might be motivated by Pat's or The Rhino's wish to start talking to me again, but this was not the case. Pat and The Rhino had their own relationship now and it did not include me.

Pat and Gwen lost no time before honoring The Rhino's request for his own room. They commissioned a local sculptor to cast him in bronze, and they redesigned the house's entryway into an elegant salon with the statue at its center. He was ceremonially installed there in March, 1986. He has been very happy to have his own space even though it does not have a water view. After being loaned to an art museum in the city for several weeks, he was so glad to get home that on the night of his return Pat dreamed he was dancing with a tambourine.

"We'll never loan him out again," she said. "He's the heart of the house."

In thirty-some years of practice I have never seen two identical dreams, but even in a field where the unique is commonplace, Pat's dreams are extraordinary. What factors would account for such a remarkable series of dreams?

Jung says that dreams usually compensate some aspect of the dreamer's conscious life. I speculate that The Rhino's dependable presence may compensate the uncertainty of a life in which death is always at hand. Just as mortally ill incubants in ancient Greece had to "live with the God" if they hoped to be cured, so Pat must live with The Rhino to go on living at all.

Beyond that is the question of what kind of person would have these dreams. The dreams themselves attest to an intelligence and psychological integrity well beyond the ordinary. Everyone has inner conflicts and splits, but Pat's are peculiarly held within the unitary but paradoxical figure of The Rhino. Most of the people who come to me are looking for help with neurotic or psychotic problems. In contrast, Pat's problems are almost entirely physical, even though they have been resolved by psychological means. Her psyche is fundamentally healthy.

Pat is extremely introverted. Her totem animal—the creature most like her conscious personality—is not the rhinoceros but the turtle, always protected by a shell. Still, she is self-possessed and straightforward, with a quick sense of humor, a strong ethical perspective, and unusual independence of thought and action. In view of the trying circumstances of her life, it is notable that I have never seen her indulge in self-pity. She has always gone steadfastly on with her life and done everything within her power to meet her myriad responsibilities. Even when she was so sick that she could barely move around, she never used The Rhino's frequent statement that "If a thing is worth doing, it's worth doing easily" as an excuse to slack off.

When I asked her how she understands this message, she said, "The Rhino is saying that if a thing is worth doing, it is worth taking the time to know it, and to let it show me how it wants to be done. He is also telling me to focus on the things that are part of the natural flow of my own life, and to forego those things that are not. He is telling me to reflect on why a thing is hard, and either to change my relationship with it or to let it go.

"He is not telling me to be a lazy bum, to skip the mundane stuff of life, or to forego intellectually or physically difficult things. He's just saying that it is not useful to keep hitting one's head against a wall. If the wall is blocking the path, find a door, build a door, or find another path."

While the Rhino's grandiosity is appropriate to a divine being, Pat resists the self-importance that easily gets the better of gifted people. She wrote the following unassuming summary of a life-history that shows the magnitude of her gifts:

"I was born in Los Angeles in 1931. My early schooling was in UCLA's teacher training school, after which, at sixteen, I entered the University of Chicago. I graduated at eighteen after a fascinating two years, including a physics course from Enrico Fermi, who had a lasting effect on me because he had a lot of regrets about the atomic bomb. He made me very concerned about at least not doing ill in the world.

"I received my Ph.D. from UCLA in philosophy (logic, set theory, foundations of mathematics), and also took the courses for an MA in math. I have been very fortunate in my education, both formal and otherwise. My mother was a librarian, so I read widely as a kid. At Chicago, I went to the Art Institute almost weekly, thus learning a lot about visual art, and living with Gwen [a musician] has been an education in music.

"I met Gwen when I was twenty-two and she was twenty, and we've lived together ever since.

"I planned to be a university professor, but don't like to teach so went into computer design instead. I was assistant director of the Health Sciences Computing Facility in the UCLA medical center and later directed the hospital's data processing department where I developed systems for handling medical orders. I retired in 1991, after working for UCLA for twenty-five years. Recently I have designed statistical software for use in clinical trials for a company in Ireland, and developed software for customizing patient instructions for a company in Port Townsend.

"I've always written—technical writing, poetry, novels, short stories. I have a strong interest in animals and nature, used to backpack a lot in the High Sierra, and have traveled twice to the Galapagos, fourteen times to Africa, and once to Australia and New Zealand.

"Since 1994, I have been an emergency medical technician. I am managing editor of a small literary magazine that Gwen and

I started and treasurer of a professional chamber orchestra we started.

"The two really negative things in my life have been rheumatic fever and my boyfriend committing suicide when I was twenty, writing me a letter which I received after I knew he was dead, blaming me. Rationally I knew it wasn't my fault, but who's rational?"

That is as much as I can tell you about what kind of person would have such remarkable dreams.

I had not seen Pat for more than eight years when, in 1999, I ran into her at a party. She was recovering from her second hip replacement and would soon have a third. The second superceded the first, which had failed, but I like to imagine that it replaced one of The Rhino's massive joints. Pat told me that for eighteen years she had avoided all physicians except the orthopedic surgeon, whom she had twice managed to convince that she had no serious heart problems. However, preparations for the third hip replacement revealed that her blood pressure was very high so she now began to see a doctor regularly again. An echocardiogram before the surgery showed that there was only a small amount of residual scarring of the valves that had once been so badly damaged, a result that would be repeated four years later.

Pat was still keeping faith with The Rhino, and doing her best to serve his needs.

"I've done almost everything he's asked," she said, "but there's one thing left. He still wants to be published."

Years before she had tried to get The Rhino dreams published. The effort was unsuccessful, I imagine because the dreams have to be seen in their psychological context to be understood. The preface Pat wrote at the time shows how important it seemed to get his message into the world:

"During my early association with The Rhino, I could tell he wanted something of me, but I didn't know what. At first I thought his message was personal—urging me to view life as a whole, not with the limited eye of my rational ego. Later I realized that he wanted to reach a wider audience. He speaks for life. All life, not just human life. The lives of animals and plants, and of the earth itself. He speaks to our desperate post-modern world, saying we must turn away from our arrogance and learn again to live with the rhinos, the crocodiles, and all the natural, instinctive forms of life—now, before they are gone, leaving us alone, alienated, and doomed to extinction."

Now that there is convincing evidence of global climate change, we are attuned to the vital importance of this message, but twenty-some years ago The Rhino was a voice in the wilderness. Pat goes on:

"At first I tried to classify The Rhino. For a while I thought he symbolized the onrushing flow of life, later the trickster, who gives us technically true but misleading answers to our most basic questions.

"Gradually I learned that he was not so easily classified, and finally that he is simply The Rhino. But I was puzzled by his urgency. He had my attention and my view of life had changed, so what did he want?

"At last, in a dream, I remembered to ask him:

I find myself at a concert in a natural grotto lighted by stars attached at intervals to the sides of the cavern.

The orchestra and chorus are performing the Messiah. The conductor is The Rhino, and the orchestra members are animals. Elephants make up the percussion section, the strings are members of the cat family—cheetahs on first violin, leopards on second, tigers playing viola, female lions on cello, and a large, lazy male lion with a black mane playing bass. Large birds compose the wind section except for the piccolos, which are small song birds. The brasses are hyenas. Soloists are a hippo, a hyena, a lion, and a cheetah. The words are about the greatness of The Rhino.

When the performance ends, the sun is turned on overhead and the auditorium becomes a desert with long grasses blowing in the wind. The orchestra members move about naturally in the sunlight.

The Rhino comes to me and asks, 'What are you doing, riding around in an auditorium seat in the middle of the Kalahari desert?'

I say, 'It was an auditorium a minute ago. What happened to the musicians?'

He answers, 'You can only see them by starlight, but they're always here in the desert.'

I say, 'I've been meaning to ask you something, but when I see you, I can never remember what it is.'

He replies, 'What I want you to do is to write about me, in a form that people will attend to. I can't do it alone. No one would listen to a rhino.'

Notwithstanding this modest assessment of his worldly power, in my experience The Rhino is a force to be reckoned with. He is so potent that whenever I write or lecture about him I feel strangely energized, my psyche so activated that I feel I must grow larger to contain what he stirs up in me. Similarly, the sculptor who rendered The Rhino in bronze became quite agitated and dreamed about The Rhino regularly until the piece was finished.

A woman who works for Pat and Gwen confided that whenever she looks at the bronze Rhino she sees him winking at her.

This is a direct expression of his numinosity. The word *numinous* derives from an Indo-European root that means "to nod," implying that at bottom a numinous experience is the sense of being acknowledged by a god. The icon nods—or winks—as a visible sign of divine recognition.

Apparently, the journey Pat has taken with The Rhino has given him a life of his own. Science cannot easily fathom such a thing, but the alchemists knew about it. They observed that once the alchemical gold was formed, it could exert its beneficial effects in the world outside the laboratory, multiplying itself like the loaves and fishes in the Christian parable. They called the effect *multiplicatio*.

The *multiplicatio* gives symbolic form to an important psychological fact: The most effective way to change the world is first to change yourself. We all have within us the ability to do evil and to do good, to kill and to heal. Which side will predominate in your life or mine depends entirely on how we relate to it. We so-called civilized people will go to almost any lengths not to become aware of that primeval power in ourselves, although we see it clearly in others and are quick to condemn or idealize it where we see it. This mechanism, called *projection*, threatens to blow the world apart unless enough people turn inward and form the right kind of relationship to the power of life and death within themselves. Then that mysterious inner other *might* find a way to heal both our individual personal wounds and also some small part of this grievously endangered planet.

The crux is the word "right." The *right* kind of relationship with the God within, which Jung calls the Self, is the hardest thing on earth to achieve. Like Pat's relationship with The Rhino, it is a lifetime task.

CHAPTER THREE

# How to Listen to The Rhino

"At first, the encounter with the Self is indeed a defeat for the ego; but with perseverance, *Deo volente* [God willing], light is born from the darkness. One meets the 'Immortal One' who wounds and heals, who casts down and raises up, who makes small and makes large—in a word, the One who makes one *whole.*"

—EDWARD F. EDINGER[19]

Almost no one else has dreams like Pat Britt's, but everyone has an inner life, often without even realizing it. Anyone who takes the ever-present inner voices and images seriously enough can develop a conscious, intentional dialogue with them. Inner conversation of this sort is the beginning of a complex process that Jung called active imagination, a method for "coming to terms with the Other in us"[20] whose facets this chapter will explore.

Active imagination is not usually undertaken until late in an analytic process, after a person has worked for years to understand dreams and the myriad ways in which the unconscious manifests in everyday life. During this time, a responsible and respectful attitude toward the world of the psyche is born and matures. Only then does it become possible to relate directly, while awake, to the characters involved in the inner drama

Active imagination calls upon all the virtues the ancients believed were needed to do the work of alchemical transformation, among them patience, courage, perseverance, and religious devotion; and the avoidance of haste, despair, and deception.[21] In fact, Jung speaks of active imagination as the closest psychological equivalent to the symbolic processes of alchemy,[22] and says that its greatest value lies in the fact that "in this way we get to know aspects of our nature which we would not allow anybody else to show us and which we ourselves would never have admitted."[23] Not many people want to be quite so well-informed about themselves, but those who do reap important benefits. At the very least, looking at what lies beneath the surface makes life interesting and meaningful. Beyond that, the process enlarges and stabilizes the personality, destroying self-congratulatory illusions and grounding the ego in dependable psychological realities.

On a more altruistic level, anyone who shoulders the burden of seeing and taking full responsibility for his own psyche can help reduce a kind of contamination of the psychological environment that we rarely acknowledge consciously. For instance, we have all experienced the shimmering intensity that falls upon a room whenever a charismatic public figure is discussed. The divine or demonic energies that such people embody belong to everyone, but only someone who has gotten acquainted with these parts of himself is in a position to counteract the poisonous atmosphere.

I was once demonized by a cult-like group of people, most of whom had never actually met me. However, I had been pointed out to them, and when I happened to pass one on the street I could feel the hostility directed at me. I learned to identify members of this group by the atmosphere they exuded, and in nearly all such cases I was eventually able to confirm the hypothesis that they were members of the cult.

A person's unintegrated emotional reaction creates a similar sort of pollution of the social atmosphere. A member of a discussion group came to a meeting in a rage, and everyone present was scorched by the emotions that smoldered in him, even though he sat in a corner and said nothing. Energies of archetypal proportions are catching. They have an inductive effect, activating similar material in others. Only the objectivity that self-knowledge makes possible can prevent a contagion.

In these ways and others, unconscious aspects of the psyche leak into the world and poison social intercourse. Working with archetypal images and emotions internally, in active imagination, averts their harmful effects, transforming material that would be destructive if taken literally and acted out concretely into meaningful, life-giving symbols.

When Jung speaks of a symbol, he means something quite specific. In his view, a living symbol gives form to something that reaches down into the roots of the psyche and cannot be expressed in any other way. If such an image is understood completely rationally, it is cut off from its emotional underpinnings and ceases to function as a living symbol. For instance, I can say that a red rose can mean passion without its having any emotional impact upon me. However, the gift of a red rose may function symbolically, serving as a bridge to a profound emotional response. Similarly, for some people, partaking of the bread and wine of the Eucharist is a living experience of Christ. For them, the consecrated food and drink constitute a true symbol.

Images that the unconscious generates spontaneously are living symbols, rooted in the irrational ground of being. Active imagination is a way to make a bridge between the world from which they come and that of ordinary reality. To relate to a symbolic image we sometimes have to "suspend disbelief," setting aside the linear reasoning of ego-consciousness. A certain amount of instinct and experience is required to know when to do that and when to insist on the truth of linear thought and cause-and-effect reasoning, so an analyst's help is advisable when a person first ventures into active imagination. Later, however, relating to the unconscious in this way can bring authentic psychological independence of the analyst, for it offers a means to explore the inner world without another person's intervention.

In the earliest and most complete paper I know about active imagination, Barbara Hannah writes:

> Whenever man has tried to come to terms with an invisible, supernatural and apparently eternal reality . . . he has instinctively evolved . . . some form of meditation or dialogue that corresponds in a greater or lesser degree with what Jung has called active imagination.[24]

Hannah's treatment of the subject in spiritual terms resonates with my own feeling that active imagination is most meaningfully described as *a dialogue with the God (or gods) within*.

One implication of this definition is that there are at least two participants, even though both reside within the same individual. The first is a conscious ego, rooted in ordinary reality. A person cannot relate meaningfully to the imaginal world unless he is separate from it and grounded in everyday life. Referring to a time when he was flooded with archetypal images, Jung says:

> Particularly at this time, when I was working on the fantasies, I needed a point of support in 'this world,' and I may say that my family and my professional work were that to me. It was most essential for me to have a normal life in the real world as a counterpoise to that strange inner world. My family and my profession remained the base to which I could always return, assuring me that I was an actually existing, ordinary person. The unconscious contents could have driven me out of my wits. But my family, and the knowledge: I have a medical diploma from a Swiss university, I must help my patients, I have a wife and five children, I live at 228 Seestrasse in Kusnacht—these were actualities which made demands upon me and proved to me again and again that I really existed, that I was not a blank page whirling about in the winds of the spirit, like Nietzsche. Nietzsche had lost the ground under his feet because he possessed nothing more than the inner world of his thought—which incidentally possessed him more than he it. He was uprooted and hovered above the earth, and therefore he succumbed to exaggeration and irreality. For me, such irreality was the quintessence of horror. . . .[25]

The other partner in the dialogue of active imagination is a discrete piece of inner life: a voice, an image, an emotion, a fragment of fantasy, a figure from a dream. Like The Rhino, the characters in the psyche are often quite numinous. That is why, in talking about active imagination, I prefer the language of religion to that of psychology. "Archetypes of the collective unconscious" is the psychological term for gods and demons, but such abstract words do not communicate anything about the actual experience. The word "God" has an emotional impact that conveys what it is really like to converse with an archetypal image. It makes the autonomy and immensity of these figures clear, and shows how important it is to pay careful attention to them, and fully respect their power.

Undertaking to communicate with the God within, without mediation by the church or even an analyst, is not for the fainthearted. Consider how hard it is to relate intimately to another human being, and how often the people we thought we knew best surprise us. Getting to know inner figures is no easier, and the difficulties are magnified in a culture such as ours that tends to discount the inner life, the invisible, and the non-rational. Active imagination requires inner relationships to be taken as seriously as outer ones, and some of the same considerations apply. For example, full regard for the separateness and idiosyncrasies of the other is essential. Like the people in our outer relationships, the figures of the unconscious cannot be forced to behave as the ego thinks they should. At the same time, when we enter the inner world it is important to hold firmly to human realities and values. All manner of things are permissible in the realm of imagination, but Godlike fantasies acted out in the outside world are responsible for unspeakable horrors.

It is as true in inner relationships as outer ones that some things are personal and private, not to be discussed indiscriminately with others. In today's climate, telling the wrong person about your interesting inner life can get you hospitalized or put on psychotropic drugs. By the same token, someone who does not understand that fantasizing something is not the same as doing it would be alarmed to hear about your murderous or sexually exploitative impulses. An important difference between people who are in mental hospitals or drugged out of their minds and those who continue to function in the world is that the latter understand who not to tell about their inner life, and also know enough not to act it out.

The crux of active imagination is the word "active." As in any relationship, if one partner does not participate actively, the other simply takes over. If the ego is passive, the person is likely to be overwhelmed by obsessive fantasies, or worse, to translate them into action. The extreme of this condition is psychosis. If, on the other hand, the ego is too dominant, the voice of the unconscious is not allowed to express itself freely and the process becomes a narcissistic monologue.

The popular culture of plays and films offers many examples of the kind of relationship to divinity that expresses itself in active imagination. In *Fiddler on the Roof*, the father Tevya carries on active, down-to-earth, no-nonsense discussions with his God. Similarly, in *Breaking the Waves*, the young woman Bess has passionate conversations with the God of her experience. Danny Boyle's *Millions* shows five-year-old Damian, whose mother has died, talking about his ethical dilemmas with a female saint, while the title figure in Neil Jordan's *The Butcher Boy* talks with the Virgin Mary. In *Donnie Darko*, the other partner in the dialogue is a human-sized, surrealistic rabbit. *Waitress* shows the protagonist pouring her heart out in letters to her unborn baby, and in *Cast Away*, the shipwrecked Chuck Nolan converses with a personified volleyball that he calls "Wilson," the name printed on the ball.

*Close Encounters of the Third Kind*, Steven Spielberg's classic science fiction film, portrays the emotional intensity of active imagination along with many details of the process. Visitors from another planet fill their human contacts with a sense of urgent necessity to paint or sculpt a picture of the mountain where the extra-terrestrials are going to land. Other people feel compelled to work out the mathematical-musical-color language that the aliens speak. These expressive forms are the only way humans can communicate with the aliens. The drive for a relationship with the inner "other" often begins in a similar way, with an urge toward some specific form of creative expression: sculpture, painting, dance, music, poetry, or even some newly evolving form.

Marie-Louise von Franz divides the process of active imagination into four steps:

1. At the beginning, the thoughts of ego-consciousness must be set aside to give the unconscious a chance to enter. She refers to this as "stopping the mad mind."
2. The unconscious comes in, in the form of fantasies, images, or emotions. These are written down or given some other concrete form, but not acted out.
3. The ego reacts to whatever has emerged.
4. Conclusions are drawn and put to work in life.[26]

At the first stage, you have to become aware that there are:

. . . two different standpoints inside. One is your conscious standpoint. You say: 'I like this.' But then a voice says: 'I don't like it.' Make that experiment, try it; it is a sort of dialectical method of finding out about your partner, your own differences. Choose a somewhat controversial object, a modern art exhibition, or the standpoint of one's wife, or of one's husband,

and ask yourself what you think or feel about it. . . . It is not necessary that anybody listens to this experiment; you can do it
for yourself in the quiet of your room. Say: 'I think such and
such'—and then listen, just cock your ears to hear whether you
hear another opinion. Instantly up it comes: 'Oh no, not at all.
I think otherwise. . . .' This possibility of a dialectical method
or a contradictory process is given by the fact that you never can
get rid of the other point of view . . . which simply expresses . . .
the opposites which are always in yourself. We hate it, but it is
nevertheless true. You cannot get rid of the opposites by saying
the other thing does not exist. It does exist, it exists first of all
in yourself, you are split from the beginning, because the hermaphroditic image of man . . . was split when you were born.
You are outside, but inside you still have the recollection of the
two . . . this side and that, the opposites.[27]

The critical, judging mode of ego-consciousness has to be set aside
to let in that other point of view. At this initial stage the ego must
cultivate something akin to the alpha state of unfocused attention,
simply observing what comes up, remaining alert and not censor-
ing anything. As Jung puts it:

"We must be able to let things happen in the psyche. . . . Consciousness is forever interfering, helping, correcting, and negating,
never leaving the psychic processes to grow in peace. . . . To begin
with, the task consists solely in observing objectively how a fragment of fantasy develops."[28]

I once had a dream describing what *not* to do at this stage. In
the dream I planted some young trees and began right away to
worry about whether enough nutrients were reaching their roots.
So I dug up the trees to see how the roots were doing! That is the
perverse helpfulness of an ego that does not trust the psyche's

natural processes and therefore interferes with the very thing it wants to nurture.

There are a number of ways to help the interfering ego get out of the way. You can take advantage of the natural state of un-focused attention that occurs during routine activities such as tooth-brushing, shaving, washing dishes, ironing, or exercising. A small notebook or tape recorder may be useful to save fragments of fantasy that you notice. Or you can do a ritual to stimulate the imaginal process. When I first began doing active imagination I would activate the unconscious by turning down the lights, light-ing a candle, and sitting in a relaxing chair. When a dream seems unfinished or there is an especially powerful dream image, it is often possible to get back into the dream and allow it to continue in waking imagination. And working with graphic or plastic ma-terial instead of words sometimes reduces the ego's interference. The hands can do what they want while the head is engaged in its own thoughts.

The appropriate attitude for the first step is that of a child at play. The hardest thing for adults to learn about play is to take it seriously. Children freely create worlds, destroy them, and create new ones. It is enormously important to be able to do this, not only for active imagination but for most creative endeavors. When I returned to graduate school as an oldster of thirty-five, I dreamed that I had to go to my childhood home and bring back a set of children's building blocks. I did not yet appreciate how vital it would be to recapture the playful-serious creative perspective the blocks represented both to facilitate my graduate work and to sus-tain my spirit in the earnest and rational scholarly environment.

At the beginning of Jung's journey into the unconscious, he re-alized that in order to go deeper he would have to play like a child:

If I wanted to re-establish contact with [my eleventh year], I had no choice but to return to it and take up once more that child's life with his childish games. This moment was a turning point in my fate, but I gave in only after endless resistances and with a sense of resignation. For it was a painfully humiliating experience to realize that there was nothing to be done except play childish games. Nevertheless, I began accumulating suitable stones, gathering them partly from the lake shore and partly from the water. And I started building: cottages, a castle, a whole village.[29]

Long after these events he wrote, "The creative activity of imagination frees man from his bondage to the 'nothing but' and raises him to the status of one who plays."[30] This is the status that must be reached for active imagination to begin.

As the voice of the unconscious emerges it has to be put into writing or some other tangible form. Otherwise it is too easy to let the images and emotions pass through without acknowledging exactly what they are, to be a little dishonest about what the voice says or what the image is or how you honestly feel. Few things are more damaging to the psyche than self-deception. You can get away with deceiving your neighbor, your spouse, or even your analyst, but self-deception gives power to the parts of yourself you are ashamed to face and puts you at their mercy.

Active imagination is defined by the relationship between ego and unconscious, not by the particular medium employed. The unconscious can express itself in many ways—through poetry, stories, dialogue, verbal description of images, sculpture, painting, dance, photographs, movies, music, or collage. Doing these things can be one step in active imagination but they are never the whole process. Deciding what medium to use is an individual matter. Whatever is comfortable at a given moment is usually fine. If you are skilled in one medium, another might work better for active imagination. The unconscious expresses itself through mistakes, and skill prevents mistakes. On the other hand, if you are afraid of the unconscious, you might be able to ease into the work by using a medium over which you have a certain amount of control.

Clay has the advantage of being down-to-earth and far from the head, making the process concrete and real. Written dialogue can facilitate cognitive understanding. In my own inner work, the medium I use depends in part on the state of the content. When I am in the grip of an emotion, I find it easiest to use a graphic or plastic material, but under other circumstances I prefer to write.

It is only at the third stage, when the ego begins to react to the images of the unconscious, that the process can properly be called active imagination. This is the time for the ego to raise questions, doubts, and reservations; to have emotional reactions and make judgments

Now the ego must become fully aware that an intangible event such as a thought, an emotional reaction, or an image is just as real in its own realm as a concrete one in ordinary reality. If a rattlesnake bites you in the outside world, pretending that it did not happen will not undo it. A rattlesnake bite in a dream or active imagination is equally irreversible, but the effects may be different from that of an outer-world bite, and different rules may apply. For instance, Edinger suggests that if you are offered something to eat in a dream—and I would add in imagination—you should always eat it, no matter how inedible, even deadly, it would be in outer reality. Similarly, if someone knocks on your psychic door, you should "open the door and show immediate hospitality, even though it is a stranger,"[31] which is not always wise in the outside world.

The figures of the unconscious express the reality of the inner world, but they are ignorant of human realities. The ego has to confront the unconscious with the requirements of life in the world as well as human limits and ethical concerns. At a time when something within me was pushing me too far beyond my capacities, I was startled to hear my analyst say, "Sometimes you have to say no to the Self." Coming from a Christian background where "thy will be done" is the ideal, I was surprised to learn that I could talk back to the gods within, even that it was necessary, and that when I did talk back, both my conscious ego and the inner demand were changed by the interaction.

Here at the third step an ethical attitude becomes imperative. Now it is time to stop watching the images passively, as if they were a movie, and to have an emotional response and make judgments about what is happening. Jung describes a situation in which the appropriate response to an inner image was lacking:

> One of my patients had the following fantasy: He sees his fiancée running down the road towards the river. It is winter, and the river is frozen. She runs out on the ice and he follows her. She goes right out, and then the ice breaks, a dark fissure appears, and he is afraid she is going to jump in. And this is what happens: she jumps into the crack and he watches her sadly.
>
> This fragment, although torn out of its context, clearly shows the attitude of the conscious mind: it perceives and passively endures, the fantasy-image is merely seen and felt, it is two-dimensional, as it were, because he himself is not sufficiently involved. Therefore the fantasy remains a flat image,

concrete and agitating perhaps, but unreal, like a dream. This unreality comes from the fact that he himself is not playing an active part. If the fantasy happened in reality he would not be at a loss for some means to prevent his fiancée from committing suicide. He could, for instance, easily overtake her and restrain her bodily from jumping into the crack. . . . The fact that he remains passive in the fantasy merely expresses his attitude to the activity of the unconscious in general: he is fascinated and stupefied by it.[32]

Ethical participation in active imagination protects the ego from inflation by the archetypes, that is, from identifying with the gods. When the ego becomes possessed by archetypal material the results can be quite destructive, as the following example shows.

For many months a professional writer had repressed the painful emotions connected with the sudden death of her analyst. Suddenly she began to write, day and night, and in the space of a few weeks had written a novel composed of the fantasies that played about the event. The material gripped her, but even as it poured out of her she could not respond emotionally.

She had a dream that gave her clear instructions to face the pain, but she was still unable to let it in. Next she was seized with fantasies of the wealth and power she expected when the novel was published. The inflation culminated in a long and painful manic episode, which the experience of her grief might have helped her avoid.

The final step of active imagination—drawing conclusions and putting them to work in life—means growing up and accepting full responsibility for what you have learned about yourself. The process that began as child's play culminates in psychological adulthood, a life lived in harmony with the worst and the best that is in you. This is the hardest part, and the step least often taken.

Following is a relatively simple illustration of the four steps of active imagination:

At a time in my life when I was physically and emotionally exhausted, I decided to make a collage. The first step was easy, for exhaustion had already produced the lowered state of consciousness that allows unconscious contents to emerge. The second step consisted of selecting some pictures to which I was strongly attracted and pasting them to a large piece of cardboard. Then—third step—I stood back and looked at what I had made. The central image was a young woman asleep in a hammock. Around her I had put pictures of sad, dark, primitive women and children, some animals, and people in introverted, prayerful, and self-reflective postures. Contemplating these images pulled me down into sadness, and I soon realized how far I had exceeded my human limits. I saw that I had been ignoring everything the pictures represented: my instincts, my dark feminine side, my playfulness, my strongly introverted nature. I understood that I needed to take time off from my work and other obligations, but the ego protested that this was impossible. My patients needed me; I had many commitments; I was indispensable.

The collage touched me deeply, and convinced me that I truly needed time to renew myself, but I did not do it. Soon a severe cold forced the fourth step upon me and I spent several days in bed. Even though I had drawn the right conclusion, I had not been able to take the ethical step of acting on what I knew. When the fourth step is not taken consciously, life is apt to take care of it, often in ways that are not so benevolent as a cold.

A number of processes bear some resemblance to active imagination but differ from it in important ways: prayer, meditation, guided fantasy, Gestalt work, and various art forms.

Traditional religions typically teach that the ego must submit to the divine will. In active imagination, on the other hand, the ego has to express its point of view fully, even though it may eventually have no choice but to submit. That is, traditional religions put a higher value on God than on the ego. This can be dangerous because it overlooks the dark side of the divine impulse, the demonic. In some religions, dogmatic exclusion of the powers of darkness serves a protective function, but the price can be high when, for instance, the demonic is then attributed to people whose religious or political beliefs are different from one's own. The goal of active imagination is for *everything* that comes up to be heard. In the absence of dogma to help choose between good and evil, it is up to the individual ego to make the crucial distinctions.

Meditation, too, resembles active imagination in some ways but not others. Traditional forms of meditation often prescribe the desired outcome, such as nirvana, the union of Shiva and Shakti, or peace of mind, and the way to get there is predetermined. The psyche's spontaneous contents are seen as nuisances at best, to be gotten out of the way in order to proceed along the path. In active imagination, the spontaneous contents *are* the path. While prayer undervalues the individual ego, meditation devalues the contents of the unconscious.

Guided fantasy differs from active imagination in offering ready-made images for a person to use instead of waiting for what emerges spontaneously. The analyst's or guide's images are thus added to a patient's inner equation, which muddies the relationship between ego and unconscious and increases the ever-present temptation for a patient to put himself totally in the hands of the analyst, giving up responsibility for her own psyche. It is easy then for the analyst to be seduced into the so-called "pride of the shaman," accepting the power that is offered by taking credit for a patient's successes. Strangely, though, he seldom correspondingly accepts blame for patients' failures! Gestalt methods differ from active imagination in yet another way. One Gestalt technique is for a dreamer to try to get into the skin of a dream image in order to understand what that image means in the psyche of the dreamer. In contrast, active imagination stresses the importance of remaining in one's own skin throughout the process. Even though pieces of the psyche can only speak through the voice or hand of the conscious ego, still the point is to differentiate oneself from the inner figures, not to become them. Only when differentiation has occurred is it possible to relate to archetypal images in a meaningful way. If Pat Britt had *become* The Rhino instead of relating to him, she would have become a monster.

Active imagination is not art, although some art is active imagination. That is, some artists grow and change through a confrontation with their work, but many do not, nor is this a necessary function of art.

Hannah speaks of active imagination as a "creative function."[33] All people have this creative possibility if they can tap it, but not everyone is meant to be an artist. Confusing the products of active imagination with art can be a serious mistake. For one thing, believing that your active imagination is art when you are not an artist can take you away from your real tasks in life. Jung speaks of a moment when he encountered this temptation, offered by the anima, the woman within him:

When I was writing down these fantasies, I once asked myself, 'What am I really doing? Certainly this has nothing to
do with science. But then what is it?' Whereupon a voice
within me said, 'It is art.' . . . I caught her and said, 'No it is
not art! On the contrary, it is nature,' and prepared myself for
an argument. . . .

If I had taken these fantasies of the unconscious as art,
they would have carried no more conviction than visual perceptions, as if I were watching a movie. I would have felt no
moral obligation toward them. The anima might then have
easily seduced me into believing that I was a misunderstood
artist, and that my so-called artistic nature gave me the right
to neglect reality. . . . Thus the insinuations of the anima, the
mouthpiece of the unconscious, can utterly destroy a man. In
the final analysis, the decisive factor is always consciousness,
which can understand the manifestations of the unconscious
and take up a position toward them.[34]

Further, when active imagination is mistaken for art, the product of work on the unconscious is likely to be valued more than
the process, and the meaning and value of active imagination are
lost. Finally, when active imagination is confused with art, the
individual with no artistic talent believes she cannot do active
imagination.

The question remains whether there is any connection at all
between active imagination and the work of an artist. A number
of factors enter into the making of an artist. At a minimum, she
must have talent, developed skills, and the drive to give form to
certain contents. It is as if the gods insist that a talent be put to
work. The artist carries something for all of us, giving public form
to emergent collective images. Active imagination gives private

form to such images, but they are apt to be more idiosyncratically personal than what the artist produces.

I have come to think of some people as creative personalities. They may or may not be artists, but are characterized by an absolute necessity to give form to inner images. Expression is therapeutic for them even if they never engage the complete dialogue that is active imagination. If they do not express, they become ill—physically, emotionally, or both. The unexpressed images act like a poison in them. These people nearly always find themselves crucified on a conflict between the requirements of everyday life and the inner demands of the spirit. This is often seen as the classic conflict of the artist, but it also occurs in the creative person who is not an artist, for creative vision is more often than not incompatible with existing collective values. The creative process produces images of new gods that challenge or destroy the old. It is easy to glorify creativity without fully appreciating how destructive new ideas can be to someone held together by the old, established ways.

Dreams of nuclear bombs, tidal waves, and earthquakes attest to the devastating destructive potential of the unconscious. Because the first step of active imagination encourages a reduction in ego control, it is potentially more dangerous than working with dreams. As Hannah points out[35], active imagination is not dangerous when it is done right, but it is hard to do right and easy to do wrong. In fact, if a person finds active imagination very easy, it may be a danger sign.

The most serious danger of this work is the possibility of losing the boundary between inner and outer reality and being overwhelmed by unconscious contents. Sometimes, when the unconscious takes over completely, there is a psychotic interval.

This is most likely to happen when a person does not know how to separate from, confront, and work with emergent contents, i.e., when he has not learned how to do active imagination. A number of patients have come to me after having fallen into the unconscious by using psychedelic drugs or some form of meditation, and active imagination has been the tool that enabled them to regain their footing. However, it is possible for even the most experienced traveler in the unconscious to be overwhelmed. Jung complained that he found American patients difficult to analyze because their psyches have not had the long historical development characteristic of Europeans. He said that Europeans descend into the unconscious in an orderly, stepwise fashion, but that Americans are always falling in.

Children, whose incompletely formed egos keep them close to the unconscious, know instinctively how important it is to maintain the boundary between inner and outer reality. When my son Nick was a child, he had an inner companion named Tiger. For years he talked to and about Tiger at every opportunity. One day I entered all the way into the game and said something about what Tiger had said to me. Nick was shocked and frightened. "Mom!" he said, "Tiger isn't *real*!"

The ego's capacity to use the power of the unconscious for ends that may not be benevolent creates another danger of active imagination. Black magic, which tries to exercise covert control over others, is an extreme form of this abuse. The power attitude fails to recognize inner figures as autonomous potencies with, in a manner of speaking, their own agendas. The psyche responds badly to this attitude, and is likely to take its revenge upon the person who tries to misuse it.

The least damaging effect of a power attitude toward the unconscious is that the ego may try to push a psychological process faster than it is ready to go, and it simply does not work. More seriously, a drive to dominate the unconscious can backfire by activating a psychosis. The only real protection from the dark side of the gods is a religious attitude that fully recognizes and respects their autonomy, power, and capacity for both good and evil.

A third danger is that symbolic material may be taken literally and acted out. To relate seriously to a fantasy of doing something is not always the same thing as doing it. A sophisticated sense of paradox is required to take the unconscious fully seriously, as something completely real in its own realm, and at the same time not to take it literally or act it out in the wrong way. Charles Manson, for example, received unconscious contents uncritically and acted them out literally. He said, "God told me to kill those people," never asking whether the word of God might not have a symbolic meaning. Similarly, terrorists in today's world often unreflectively act out what they believe to be God's will.

On the other hand, sometimes taking a fantasy seriously does mean living it in concrete reality. Discerning the difference is rarely simple, and only becomes possible at all when the inner material is carefully considered in the light of human values.

Inflation by, identification with, or possession by, unconscious contents is another danger of active imagination. A special case of this problem is to identify with the product when a content has been given a beautiful form, as when an artist identifies with his work. It is important to realize that the products of creativity stem from the divine creative power within, and are only shaped by the ego. Some artists and writers are clearly aware of this. Robert Louis Stevenson, for example, spoke of the little men inside his head who did his writing. Those who fail to make this differentiation suffer the agonies of divinity such as crucifixion, flaying, or having one's liver consumed by birds of prey. To identify with a work of art is similar to identifying with our children, not fully appreciating that what came out of us now has its own separate identity. Hitler became identified with the unconscious of a whole nation,[36] and in doing so became a living myth. Such a person is extremely charismatic because the content that possesses him has the magnetic power of a god.

Fortunately, unpleasant, unattractive contents are as common as beautiful ones. While you may be tempted to claim a beautiful poem as yours but to believe that the black witch who reared her ugly head came from somewhere else, good sense makes it clear that both are from the same source. Knowing this makes it easier not to identify with either.

Even though active imagination has its dangers, it does not *create* dangerous contents. Archetypal contents are already present in the psyche, and have an effect whether or not they are seen. Nevertheless, focusing on a particular image can, in a manner of speaking, heat up the energy behind it. Once an archetype is activated, it is more dangerous to remain unconscious of it than to meet it in active imagination, confront it with human values, and take responsibility for its effects.

Resistance to doing active imagination should be taken seriously because it is the healthy personality's natural protection against the dangers of the process. However, the person who really needs to do this work eventually has to overcome what Jung called "the damnedest lousy excuses," such as "I have no time," "I have no talent," and "I'm just making it up."

Valid resistances stem from the legitimate fear that the ego will be swamped. A woman fears that if she lets herself know how angry she is with her husband, she will have to leave him. Or she might be forced to give up her idealized view of him and learn to live with a less-than-perfect being. It is hard work to carry a fantasy and allow yourself to be changed by it without turning it loose on the world, but awareness of a fantasy or emotion is often the only thing that keeps it from taking over willy-nilly.

Lousy excuses stem from various sources: disbelief in the reality of the psyche, a perception that active imagination is incredibly hard work, a misunderstanding of what the process is, or a mistaken attitude or expectation about it. A person may have the idea that active imagination is art and that what comes out should be beautiful; or the belief that it is nothing but play, and that grownups should not play. A person may not fully realize that the process is what counts, not the product. She may identify too much with what emerges from the unconscious, failing to understand its "otherness," which makes it doubly difficult to look at embarrassing or otherwise unacceptable contents.

My first attempts to do active imagination were miserable failures. I would sit unproductively in front of my typewriter for hours. I simply could not get the hang of it. Then one day I saw an image of another "me" sitting to the left of me. She was talking, so I listened and began to write down what she was saying. She had a great deal to say about how absurd this whole business of active imagination was. She *was* the resistance. She was a woman of her culture, a thoroughgoing scientific materialist who wanted nothing to do with such an irrational process. Until that moment I had been identical with her. As long as that was true, I could not hear what she was saying, confront it, or go beyond it. I had to come to terms with her before I could go deeper into the process.

Sometimes active imagination culminates in the stable, enduring presence of an inner partner. For Pat Britt this was The Rhino, and he sprang unasked-for from her damaged heart. Usually the inner other does not become conscious so easily, but must be invited in and cultivated with great care.

Freeing the spirit from sickness, as Pat did, is a special case of active imagination. To enter voluntarily into such a process, the patient must replace the first step of active imagination with a specific focus, imagining the sickness where it is located in the body, either seeing it as a visual image or hearing it speak. It must be allowed to be or to say anything at all, no matter how odd the communication may be. Your symptoms are a potential friend, not an enemy to be destroyed, for they speak with the voice of a vital spirit that is asking for attention. If you can let it speak to you, and give it what it needs, you will have it as an inner partner for the life that remains to you, however short or long that may be. Then you may find yourself in

> . . . the state of someone who, in his wanderings among the mazes of his psychic transformation, comes upon a secret happiness which reconciles him to his apparent loneliness. In communing with himself he finds not deadly boredom and melancholy but an inner partner; more than that, a relationship that seems like the happiness of a secret love, or like a hidden springtime, when the green seed sprouts from the barren earth, holding out the promise of future harvests.[37]

In short, like Pat Britt, you may find yourself reborn.

CHAPTER FOUR

# Teresa

"Just as there is a passion that strives for blind unrestricted life, so there is a passion that would like to sacrifice all life to the spirit because of its superior creative power. This passion turns the spirit into a malignant growth that senselessly destroys human life."

—C. G. JUNG[38]

Sometimes freeing the spirit is healing, but it also can be incredibly destructive. The German fairytale "The Spirit in the Bottle" shows both sides:

Once upon a time there was a poor woodcutter. He had an only son, whom he wished to send to [the university]. However, since he could give him only a little money to take with him, it was used up long before [graduation]. So the son went home and helped his father with the work in the forest. Once, during the midday rest, he roamed the woods and came to an immense old oak. There he heard a voice calling from the

ground, 'Let me out! Let me out!' He dug down among the
roots of the tree and found a well-sealed glass bottle from
which, clearly, the voice had come. He opened it and instantly
a spirit rushed out and soon became half as high as the tree.
The spirit cried in an awful voice: 'I have had my punishment
and I will be revenged! I am the great and mighty spirit Mercurius, and now you shall have your reward. Whoso releases
me, him I must strangle.

So as soon as the boy sets the spirit free it threatens to destroy
him. It is not going to yield up its healing powers so easily. Something else has to happen first. The story goes on:

This made the boy uneasy and, quickly thinking up a trick, he
said, 'First I must be sure that you are the same spirit that was
shut up in that little bottle.' To prove this, the spirit crept back
into the bottle. Then the boy made haste to seal it and the
spirit was caught again. But now the spirit promised to reward
him richly if the boy would let him out. So he let him out and
received as a reward a small piece of rag. Quoth the spirit: 'If
you spread one end of this over a wound it will heal, and if
you rub steel or iron with the other end it will turn into silver.'
Thereupon the boy rubbed his damaged axe with the rag, and
the axe turned to silver and he was able to sell it for [a lot of
money]. Thus father and son were freed from all worries. The
young man could return to his studies, and later, thanks to his
rag, he became a famous doctor.[39]

The boy in the story has a kind of street-smarts of the spirit that
protects him from the power that he has innocently unleashed. In
ordinary reality, this level of psychological intelligence is rare. Pat

Britt has it, but only now, thirty-some years later, can I be certain that her relationship with The Rhino—the spirit released from her illness—has had unequivocally beneficial effects. The consequences of a lengthened life are not always so favorable. A premature death, which we usually assume to be tragic, may sometimes prevent even greater harm; while the cure that we think of as good can ultimately lead to undesirable consequences. For instance, the early death of someone with the capacity to become a serial killer might not be a tragedy for society; while the megalomania that sometimes accrues to a life mysteriously spared can cause enormous damage. For anyone who is deeply self-reflective, questions about the ultimate value of one's life arise in the ordinary course of events. The balance of good and evil remains uncertain until a person's last breath, a reality to which the archetypal image of the Last Judgment attests. The outcome may depend, finally, upon the level of consciousness achieved.

Many years have passed since my work with Teresa. I still think about her sometimes, wondering what the upshot of her life will be. She came to mind again the other day, when Pat Britt told me about being called to help rescue a woman who tried to climb some rickety stairs down an eighty-foot bluff to the beach, slipped on a broken board and fell to the rocks below. "It's a miracle that she only broke her leg," said Pat. The other miracle was that Pat, at twice the age of the other women EMTs, was the only one with the strength, stamina, and skill to climb down and help the men get the injured woman out.

While she was describing this incident, I felt as if I had walked into a time warp. Several years earlier, Teresa had told me about falling and hurting herself under nearly identical conditions. There were a lot of similarities between Teresa and Pat. Both were high-functioning people in prestigious positions, and each had re-covered from a life-threatening illness that released an extremely large spirit. However, there were important differences, too. Pat was well into the second half of life when I met her, and she had an authentically religious attitude toward her psychological process and the miraculous things that happened. She was not conventionally religious, but gave serious consideration and re-spect to the numinous factors in her psyche and her life.

When I met Teresa, on the other hand, she had not yet achieved the psychological maturity required to take her power-ful spirit in hand. She seemed to be identified with it, swept away and chronically unable to distinguish between herself and a su-perhuman being. Teresa's accident and the one in which Pat was called to help are like dream images that highlight the differences between the two women. Pat was able to negotiate a precarious descent to assist someone who had overestimated her capacities; while in Teresa's case, she herself was the one who overstepped.

While still an undergraduate at Harvard, Teresa had devel-oped a dangerous and invasive form of cancer, which went into remission with standard medical treatment. After she got well, she changed her major from the arts and literature to pre-med and went on to medical school. During her internship at Stanford, the cancer recurred. Again in remission, she finished the internship, moved to the Pacific Northwest, set up a family medical practice on one of Western Washington's many islands, and began to travel weekly to Port Townsend for analysis. That was when I first met her. She was thirty-six years old.

During the first year of our work, Teresa had several acci-dents, two quite serious. Once she inexplicably fell and broke her leg. Another time she impulsively turned off the lights of her car late at night, missed a curve, and crashed. I breathed a sigh of relief when there were no accidents or life-threatening illnesses during the second or third years of our work. The fall to the beach would only happen later.

Meanwhile, the young physician was busy with her practice. Her extreme idealism made her the kind of doctor who would do almost anything to help her patients. She talked to each person at length, researched puzzling symptoms, and frequently checked on patients by phone, making herself available day and night. The trouble is, her helpfulness was not exactly a conscious choice. She was driven to it, forced by her own exalted standards to give more of herself than a human being possibly could. Eventually I realized that she was in the grip of the rescue triangle.

The rescue triangle, first described by transactional analysts, comprises three roles: rescuer, persecutor, and victim. The compulsion to rescue other people whether or not help is requested, wanted, or needed is limited by the fact that people who do too much for others without adequate compensation often wind up feeling used and victimized. Rescuers who do not become conscious of this dynamic are likely, eventually, to turn the tables and attack the people they have insisted on helping. The attempt to recover what they have too freely given away turns them into persecutors. In relationships dominated by the rescue triangle, the roles of rescuer, persecutor, and victim keep moving around, creating all the permutations possible among the people involved.

I see the rescue triangle as a concrete enactment of the Judeo-Christian God-image: The God of the Old-Testament alternately rescues and persecutes His people, while Christ is both rescuing savior and sacrificial victim. Although the compulsion to identify with these roles is not confined to paid helpers, it is a definite occupational hazard for people who, like Teresa, are in a helping profession.

Teresa had barely started her practice when she was besieged by emotionally hungry patients eager to take advantage of her over-generous spirit. She was by no means the only physician on the island, but she could not or would not turn anyone away and was soon working around the clock. Whether or not she had time for a new patient or even whether she was qualified to deal with a particular problem appeared to be irrelevant. She was convinced that a physician *must* help anyone who asks. She also had idealistic beliefs about helping the poor that conflicted with the not-so-idealistic reality that she did not want to be poor herself. I sometimes twitted her by calling her Mother Teresa, something that, in retrospect, I wonder whether might have been too cruel. I took every opportunity to put her feet to the fire because I was afraid she would die unless she could become conscious far more quickly than is usual for someone so young.

Many of Teresa's patients were economically and socially deprived. She complained that the majority of problems for which they consulted her were psychosocial, not medical, but she was reluctant to refer them to the island's psychotherapists, whom she considered incompetent.

Teresa was not trained to do psychotherapy, but the psyche fascinated her and the compulsion to relieve her patients' distress seduced her into trying to treat them herself. She read some Jungian books and undertook a naive, intuitive version of what she imagined I was doing with her, optimistically projecting her own considerable potential on her patients, many of whom were trapped in a morass of poverty, substance abuse, and crime. I urged her to get the training and supervision she needed to do competent psychotherapy. She made several half-hearted efforts in that direction but stopped them all with the conviction that she knew more than her teachers.

I worried that her identification with the spirit, which kept her in a chronic state of inflation, might cause harm not only to herself but also to her patients. She was like nothing so much as a suicide bomber in the passionate grip of extreme religious ideals. I was reminded of Jung's remark:

> The danger inherent in the spirit is that it will uproot man, bear him away from the earth and inspire him to . . . flights [like that of Icarus], only to let him plunge into the bottomless sea.[40]

As if she were not busy enough, once a week Teresa traveled for several hours to work at a halfway house for recently released young criminals. In time I became aware that delinquent adolescents were numinous to her.

The landscape of Teresa's outer life was a mirror of her psyche. Behind her drive to rescue others was the despair and rage of the impoverished patients and violent criminals locked up in her own soul. Her psyche longed for her time and attention, but even when she began to understand this intellectually, she could not limit her practice to make room for herself. The victim of her own charisma, she was left without time to self-reflect or even to write down her dreams.

It took me a long time to realize that an unconscious compulsion to commit small crimes, perhaps even larger ones, was behind Teresa's fascination with criminals. When I raised questions about her entering a vacant house through an open window, playing the piano there, and taking some pots from the porch when she left, she said, "It didn't hurt anybody. Nobody wanted those pots." After accumulating so many speeding tickets that she almost lost her driver's license she said, "I don't care what the speed limit is. It's silly to go so slow on that road." Admitting that she did not believe that the rules of ordinary society applied to her, she came perilously close to an act of sexual misconduct whose consequences could easily have destroyed her life and that of the patient who was the object of her attraction—an adolescent sex offender less than half her age.

I see Teresa's fascination with her criminal patients as one facet of her fusion with the Christian archetype, for in the context of the time in which he lived, Jesus was a criminal, crucified between two thieves. Teresa had been raised a Catholic and had powerful memories of sitting alone in the church, staring at a crucifix and feeling Christ looking back at her. She no longer subscribed consciously to Christian beliefs, but at some point, probably quite early, she lost the distinction between herself and Christ.

The compulsion to play God developed at her mother's knee. The oldest of five children, she was the only girl and her parents idolized her. Her mother was seriously disturbed, her father, stern, rigid, and overly concerned with the appearance of propriety. Because the family was wealthy and socially ambitious, Teresa thought of herself as advantaged and believed that her childhood was ideal. For a long time she seemed to float above reality, cut off from any emotional reaction to what had actually happened.

The mother had a breakdown after the youngest son was born. From then on Teresa, who was not yet seven, was regularly summoned to her mother's bedroom to comfort her and, as Teresa put it, "talk her down" from psychotic intervals. Her mother would babble incoherently, with eyes rolled back as if she were having a seizure. Sometimes she talked to the child about wanting to commit suicide, or how disappointed she was with her husband. At other times, she grabbed the sewing scissors and tried to stab herself. Once she bit the little girl, and once Teresa awoke to see her father wresting a kitchen knife from her mother, who was trying to kill the baby.

Adored as much by her brothers as by her parents, the golden girl was savior to the whole family. The role made her vulnerable to the other parts of the rescue triangle as well. Victim and persecutor built up steam in the unconscious and surfaced in our work. Teresa spent many analytic hours engulfed in self-pity, the very image of the innocent victim. Slowly she became aware that when she felt this way she wanted to die, a wish that had once only expressed itself unconsciously, in illnesses and accidents. Awareness of how angry she was took longer, but in time she became inflamed with the rage that had been repressed since childhood. Three years into our work, she called to ask for an emergency appointment, saying that she wanted to kill a colleague who had treated her badly, and was afraid that if she happened to see him she might actually do it. I hoped she could integrate enough of her anger to use it consciously as the motive power required to assert her needs and set limits in her practice. She made a little progress in that direction, but she fell back into savior mode when the rage dissipated.

On a Sunday afternoon three months later, Teresa called me from her office and told me she wanted to burn down the building and to kill herself, the rage alternately turning outward and inward against herself. She had never before openly expressed a wish to end her life.

It was the late 1990s and, for a week or more preceding this phone call, the United States had been gearing up for a strike on Iraq. Saddam Hussein capitulated, and the violent energy set in motion in the collective psyche had no place to go. I mention this because Teresa was extremely sensitive to the psychic atmosphere, and this may have been one of the factors that helped trigger her rage at that moment.

There was something else, too. The day she called me a physician of her acquaintance went home from a movie and hacked his wife to death with an ax. Teresa was especially shaken when she heard about it because she recognized some of her own traits in this man. She described what a wonderful person he appeared to be, how devoted to his patients, and how kind he had been to her, offering to help her when she hadn't even asked.

The coincidence between the time of the murder and Teresa's rage was especially striking because immediately before he did it, the murderer had seen the movie *Titanic* with which Teresa felt deeply connected. Several years before the James Cameron film was made, the first dream Teresa brought to analysis—the so-called initial dream which often prefigures the course of the analytic work—took place on a large ocean liner. There was a terrible storm, the ship began to sink, and Teresa and a man friend jumped off and started to swim to shore.

The friend in Teresa's dream was another idealistic young physician like her. The image of the old-time family physician who gives unstintingly of himself seems unable to survive at a time when the financial well-being of insurance companies increasingly dictates medical decisions. Teresa and her friend were profoundly disillusioned with medicine, and both thought of leaving it. I thought the sinking ship might represent the behemoth of the medical establishment and wondered if Teresa might need to find a more individual way to practice. On the other hand, she might have to leave the field entirely. After all, she had only taken up medicine after it saved her life. Did she have a real calling as a physician, or had the rescue archetype seduced her away from her authentic path? The evening after our Sunday phone conversation, Teresa visited friends in a house on a bluff high above the water, then started down a precarious set of steps to the beach. To complete the descent safely, she should have pulled down a second set of steps at the end of the first. Instead, like the woman that Pat Britt rescued, she inadvertently stepped into space. She landed on a broken bottle, slashing her right hand, wrist, and arm, a serious injury that might have left her permanently impaired. She had stopped thinking consciously about cutting her wrists, but the impulse had still found a way to express itself.

Finally Teresa felt that she would have to abandon her overblown practice, but more blood had to be shed before she could actually make the sacrifice, once in a dream, and once in a horrifying incident in the emergency room.

In the dream, she is required to live on a small ship with incarcerated adolescent boys. She likes it there because she enjoys the boys, who are honest and angry, and because she has time to herself. At first the boat is on the ocean, then it moves into a lake, and finally it travels up a river into the wilderness. The river keeps narrowing until the boat can go no farther and Teresa, her friend John, and two or three boys get out and walk.

Dreams of a route that gets narrower and narrower until the dreamer has to proceed on foot are quite common in analysis.

They express what happens in a dialogue with the unconscious, which leaves a person less and less room for deviation from his authentic individual path.

The dream goes on:

> We walk through the woods until we come to a road. Several men with shotguns are herding a young grizzly bear toward a truck. I hope against hope that they aren't going to kill the animal. It is bellowing and screaming and trying to fight but there are too many men. They pin him against the truck and one man takes out a large knife and cuts his right jugular. Blood spills everywhere.
>
> I almost throw up. John goes over to get a better look and I scream 'Don't go! They're dangerous!' But he has already gone.
>
> The men drag John into the truck. They don't want witnesses of the bear slaughter. Then they catch me and the boys and we are their prisoners. I suspect they will kill me if I don't find a way to escape, but I can't make a plan. I am angry with John for putting us in this position.

As mentioned earlier, von Franz suggests that the right relationship to the animal soul is decisive in the conflict between good and evil. The difference between Pat Britt's relationship to The Rhino and Teresa's to the bear is illustrative. Even though Teresa is extraordinarily disturbed by the threat to the bear, she makes no effort to save the animal, despite her compulsion to rescue people in the outside world. The essential act of courage and commitment to the powerful inner figure does not take place. This contrasts sharply with Pat's attitude toward The Rhino: In her initial dream and ever after, she has seized the dangerous animal by its horn and held it.

Teresa described her friend John as a duty-bound, perfectionist physician. As she spoke of the men pinning the bear to the truck, she put her arms in the position of the crucified Christ, a hint that the bear is a primitive God-image, one that has yet to undergo a necessary transformation. Synchronistically, I had recently read about the berserkers, Teutonic men who dressed in bearskins and cultivated ecstatic rage as part of their initiation into independent adulthood. Teresa had not yet reached this level of psychological development.

Teresa felt that the dream meant she had to leave her practice. She cried and cried, in sympathy with the bear and with all the patients she would have to disappoint. She continued to cling to her practice for three more weeks. Then, on a night when she was on duty in the emergency room, the parents of a beautiful two-year-old boy brought him in, dead on arrival, with a fractured skull and multiple bruises. It was, said Teresa, the worst child abuse she had ever seen. She handled the case with cool professionalism, but found in it a powerful message.

"I'll never do that to the child in myself again," she said, and a few days later announced that she was leaving her practice. It remained to be seen whether she could become separate enough from the Christ-image to carry her gifts more consciously. If not, I feared that she was in severe danger, if not of suicide or a fatal accident then of a recurrence of her cancer.

When I work with someone who has cancer, I sometimes say that my goal is to drive her crazy. I am only half joking. The psyche in many cancers, especially in young people, looms very large, and when it is released from the body, the person's psychic pain can become so great that she does, indeed, go a little crazy for a while. Jung suggests that when we get sick we should be grateful to the body for carrying pain that is greater than the psyche can bear.

For the first thirty-some years of her life, Teresa's suffering was carried almost exclusively by her body. When she began analysis, she stopped getting sick but had a series of accidents. Later, as she became more conscious, the pain she felt primarily as rage and self-pity stopped manifesting physically.

Edinger writes that the theme of clinging to something too big for the ego often comes up in the psychology of cancer patients.[41] In my experience this often takes the form of an inability to let go of an exaggerated perfectionism or some other larger-than-life identity. A young doctor starting his first practice in Port Townsend suddenly developed a fast-spreading cancer that killed him in a few months. From the newspaper reports I inferred that his patients and everyone around him virtually worshipped him, and of course this was also true of Teresa. Members of the Kennedy family, about whom Teresa often dreamed, carry a similarly tragic charisma. The proliferation of cancer cells, beyond the control of the body's regulating centers, is a striking physical parallel to what happens in the psyche when the rescue triangle or some other godlike process rages unconsciously out of control.

For Teresa, sacrificing her titanic medical practice looked like a step in the right direction. I hoped she would then find a way to pick up her own cross in place of Christ's, shouldering her own personal life with its painful human limitations instead of trying to be a godlike being.

For a time this appeared to be happening. The injury to her hand made Teresa aware that the Self—the God within—is neither an abstraction nor something that the ego can legitimately exploit, but an objective reality to which the ego must submit. She

had imagined she could do anything she wanted, despite mount-
ing evidence that something else was in charge. After she relin-
quished her overblown practice, a non-ego center emerged as a
separate presence in her dreams. In one, she became aware of a
small child in a corner of the room, happily playing in a bubbling
circular pool. In another she was in the forest, looking into a deep
pond. Way down at the bottom was a flower, a lotus or a water
lily, waiting to unfold.

I do not know the end of this story. The flower at the bottom
of the pond is a beautiful image of the Self, but it is a picture of
potentiality, not yet born into conscious life. A profound act of
self-reflection—gazing into the depths of the pond in the
woods—would be necessary for Teresa to see the Self at all. Its
emergence and unfolding would require ongoing devotion to the
task of self-development. However, soon after this dream, Teresa
stopped analysis and took a prestigious job as medical director for
a cluster of halfway houses for delinquent adolescents. She felt
that the new job precluded seeing me during the hours that I
work, and I was not willing to accommodate her schedule by seeing her on weekends.

In the dream Teresa brought to her last session, she was pi-
loting an airplane and had to land it. Although it was one of the
hardest things she had ever done, she brought it down success-
fully. The dream gave me hope that, unlike Icarus, who fell from
the heights and died, Teresa might eventually come safely to earth.

Outside the dream, it took a long time for the plane to land.
A year after her analysis ended, Teresa called and again requested
a weekend appointment, wanting to talk about a serious problem
confronting her in working as a therapist with "a few young
women." With a heavy heart, I told her that I still did not work on

weekends. I was sorely tempted to come to her rescue, but hoped that my refusal might coax her spirit into a human-sized container where it could help her achieve her wish to be a therapist legitimately. Perhaps this is what happened. Some time later she went back to school and began a rigorous training program for the work she longed to do.

The process of being healed in body and soul cannot happen only on weekends. It is a way of being in the world, of living your life, directed from an inner center that is the compass for everything you do. Once the ego has found its right relationship to the spirit set free, the spirit, like The Rhino, must be given the best room in the house. Nothing else belongs in the center—not money or a job, not an impressive reputation, not the compulsion to solve other people's problems. The spirit demands whatever is necessary, and this may be quite different from what you want or expect. It requires, as T. S. Eliot put it:

> A condition of complete simplicity
> (Costing not less than everything)
> And all shall be well and
> All manner of things shall be well
> When the tongues of flame are in-folded
> Into the crowned knot of fire
> And the fire and the rose are one.[42]

CHAPTER FIVE

# The Paradoxical God of Violence

The only thing that really matters now is whether man can
climb up to a higher moral level, to a higher plane of consciousness, in order to be equal to the superhuman power
which [is now in] his hands. But he can make no progress with
himself unless he becomes very much better acquainted with
his own nature. Unfortunately, a terrifying ignorance prevails
in this respect, and an equally great aversion to increasing the
knowledge of his intrinsic character.

—C. G. JUNG[43]

North Americans are famously idealistic. Our cultural images of what people are supposed to be have become increasingly constricted and constricting, until we have
little room left for anything less perfect than a consistently smil-
ing face, a well-adapted extraverted persona, a thoroughly de-
odorized body, and a white, perfectly regular set of teeth. Our ideas
about what life should be no longer leave room for the terrible realities of pain and suffering, anxiety, rage, name-calling, violent

fantasies, fist-fights on the playground, barroom brawls, adolescent talk of death and destruction, terrorism, and war.

The discrepancy between the way people are and the way we want them to be and sometimes try to force them to be has created a vast split in the American psyche. To some extent we are all like Teresa, torn between perfectionist ideals and the reality of what a person can be or achieve. All the while that we identify with divine goodness, a rage-filled counter-personality builds up energy in the unconscious, like a caged rhinoceros waiting to charge. That is why a person who appears to be as virtuous as a saint can suddenly turn into the opposite, even exploding into violent crime.

So it is that today, the parts of the psyche that idealism tries so hard to repress, deny, and control, to legislate out of existence or to annihilate with psychoactive drugs, are asserting their right to exist in the most horrifying ways: the violent crimes of children; the malevolent destruction of cherished cultural monuments; religiously motivated terrorism by idealistic young people willing to die for their cause—in these ways and many others the devalued and rejected parts of the human psyche are fighting for their lives.

If we want to come to terms with violence, we must look it square in the face. We cannot turn our backs on the dark side of human nature or pretend that it is possible or even desirable to get rid of it once and for all. The most we can hope for is that a few people—enough to make a difference—may be ready and able to contain and examine their violent impulses and, having faced and taken responsibility for their own, to stand up effectively to the violence of others. The terrible events of September 11, 2001, and the ensuing years show all too well how little we can afford to be innocent of these painful realities. As Jung so cogently put it,

"The world hangs by a thin thread, and that thread is the psyche of man."[44]

As early as 1951, Jung foresaw the predicament that the turn of the century would bring:

> ...The approach of [the eon of] Aquarius will constellate the problem of the union of opposites. It will then no longer be possible to write off evil as the mere privation of good; its real existence will have to be recognized. This problem can be solved neither by philosophy, nor by economics, nor by politics, but only by the individual human being via his experience of the living spirit.[45]

After commenting on the problem of evil in Christian theology, he segues into a discussion of contemporary life:

> The less [the devil] is recognized the more dangerous he is. Who would suspect him under those high-sounding names of his, such as public welfare, lifelong security, peace among the nations, etc.? He hides under idealisms, under isms in general, and of these the most pernicious is doctrinarism, that most unspiritual of all the spirit's manifestations. The present age must come to terms drastically with the facts as they are, with the absolute opposition that is not only tearing the world asunder politically but has planted a schism in the human heart. We need to find our way back to the original, living spirit which, because of its ambivalence, is also a mediator and uniter of opposites. . . .[46]

Just as, in Biblical times, God spoke to Moses from a bush that burst unexpectedly into flame, so today the spirit expresses itself in shocking ways. As Edinger points out[47], we live in an apocalyptic time. Like Revelation's angels, young people in suburban North America and terrorists throughout the world are "emptying bowls of God's anger over the earth."[48]

I am not suggesting that reading scripture drives people to mass murder. I am saying that a powerful archetype is activated, the same one that touched the author of the Biblical book of Revelation during the *last* change in eons more than 2000 years ago. When an archetype is activated, certain stereotyped patterns are set in motion automatically unless human consciousness intervenes. An individual who can understand the value, meaning and purpose of an archetypal event instead of acting on it has the power to transform a certain amount of archetypal energy or divert it into less destructive channels.

Activated archetypes have a powerful inductive effect, which may be why criminal violence tends to be contagious. Contemporary thought about violent crime uses ideas from the field of epidemiology to explain why homicides, for example, spread through populations in the particular way that they do. When the number of murders in an area increases, the quantity does not grow in linear fashion, but typically "tips over" from a constant rate of growth to a major outbreak. This and other psycho-social aspects of violent crime behave so much like viral infections that the Centers for Disease Control in Atlanta have a violence epidemiology branch to identify the symptoms of the "disease" of homicide and apply the theory of epidemics to its spread.[49]

You can observe the contagiousness of violent emotions yourself. If you are in a group of people when a controversial idea is discussed, notice how quickly one person's rage can trigger something like the wrath of God in everyone in the room. Simply talking about an archetypal subject like violence can activate the thing itself, but consciousness of this dynamic can moderate its effect.

The understanding of violence from a depth-psychological perspective can benefit greatly from some familiarity with the concepts of ego and Self as Jung described them. Other approaches to psychology use these words differently, and everyday street usage is different too. Jung describes the ego as the subjective center of conscious awareness and personal identity. The ego is grounded in the realities, limitations, and values of human life. The naive ego is unaware of the existence of the Self or even of the unconscious, but believes it (the ego) is the whole person.

The Self, in Jung's terminology, is the unconscious regulating center of the total personality including both consciousness and the unconscious. Like a kind of psychological DNA, the Self carries the innate ground plan for a person's individual development. Self is often spelled with a capital "S" to indicate that its energy and authority are so great that we experience it as if it were God; in fact, Jungians sometimes use Self as a synonym for God, although strictly speaking it only refers to the *image* of God in the psyche. Like the Old-Testament Yahweh, the God of the Apocalypse, and even like The Rhino, the Self is filled with contradictions. In its raw, unaltered form, it is unpredictable, amoral, demanding, perplexing, burdensome, and frequently violent. However, when the ego is out of touch with the Self, life lacks meaning and vitality.

Edinger suggests that the Self is calling attention to itself on a large scale today. It is as if, in this interesting time in which we are living, God were trying to incarnate in all humanity. The men who piloted planes into the World Trade Center and the Pentagon were filled with divine righteousness and wrath. If their egos

THE PARADOXICAL GOD OF VIOLENCE

85

had been more developed, they might have confronted the primitive energy in themselves and found less destructive ways to express it. I am reminded of a song by Flanders and Swann in which a young cannibal confronts his elders, saying, "Don't eat people. Eating people is wrong," and sticks to it despite his parents' protest that "People have always eaten people!" Like the ego confronting the Self, the youngster hopes to change primitive, stereotyped patterns so embedded in the psyche that we feel they have been there "always."

When I began to reflect about the problem of violence, I was soon forced to face the fact that violence is not all bad. In fact, the word "violent" is rooted in the Indo-European *wei-*, which means "vital force." Since one definition of the word God is "an immanent vital force," the etymology hints at a close relationship between violence and God. Only two other English words have grown from the same root: "vim" and "violate," which are opposite in feeling tone. Another Indo-European root *wiros*, meaning "man," is also thought to be related to violence, and its cognates are similarly divided between positive characteristics, like "virility" and "virtue," and words with such unpleasant connotations as "werewolf" and "virago."[50] Clearly, the idea that violence is an attribute of divinity and has elements of both good and evil is deeply embedded in our language.

It should not be a surprise, then, that the Self often breaks into consciousness in ways that are violent, primitive, even monstrous. It makes itself known as a gashed hand or a life-threatening illness, a dream of a grizzly bear or a charging rhinoceros, as often as in the image of a water lily or a beautiful child. In any deep analysis there are violent moments that seem essential to the healing process. Only when an analyst is comfortable enough with the violent side of human nature to provide a strong container for it can he or she help patients with what Jung saw as the millennial task: carrying the divine opposites of good and evil within the individual.

A nearly superhuman effort is required to see and bear the reality of good and evil simultaneously. Jung puts it this way: "the good man succumbs to evil, the sinner is converted to good, and that, to an uncritical eye, is the end of the matter. [However], the one-after-another [first good, then evil, or vice versa] is a bearable prelude to the deeper knowledge of the side-by-side, for this is an incomparably more difficult problem. . . . The view that good and evil are spiritual forces outside us, and that man is caught in the conflict between them, is more bearable by far than the insight that the opposites are the ineradicable and indispensable preconditions of all psychic life, *so much so that life itself is guilt.*"[51]

Today we are so imbued with the notion that we can and should avoid guilt, by being good and eschewing evil, that it is extraordinarily difficult to grasp what Jung is saying here. First we have to understand that we cannot be entirely good, no matter how hard we try, because everything we do has both good and evil consequences. Then it is necessary to *see* the good and evil in what we do instead of repressing or denying the bad. For instance, helping my son out of a financial bind is a generous act *and* it belittles his ability to deal with his own problems. Similarly, having my cat put down is an act of kindness that will save him from the agony of multiple surgeries or a slow, painful death; *and at the same time* I have to acknowledge that I am killing him because I do not want the trouble and expense of keeping him alive. Finally, after seeing the dark side of what we do, we have to carry the guilt instead of trying to make it look good.

This has important implications for dealing with the problem of violence. Allan Guggenbuhl has described a promising approach to classroom crisis intervention that gives the dark side of the psyche its due.[52] His team in Bern, Switzerland, is called in when a teacher reaches the end of her rope with an out-of-control class. Everyone who has anything to do with the class is required to participate in the intervention: school administrators, teachers, parents, and all the students in the offending classroom. Blame placing is avoided, and everyone involved is expected to help solve the problem.

The children are told that their class has been identified as a violent one. They are all held responsible, even if only one or two students have been misbehaving. Members of the intervention team read horrifying stories and fairy tales to the class and, in this way, says Guggenbuhl, "the *terrible* in human existence is consciously brought into school. Only through confrontation with our ugly sides can we hope that they will not control us." He concludes, "Violence and aggression in school can only be overcome *with* the students and not *against* them. A crisis intervention seeks to help the children fortify themselves to give them the ability to take on the problems of violence and aggression."[53]

This is quite contrary to enormous efforts in this country to protect children from knowledge of or responsibility for horrible things. Within a year of the massacre at Columbine High School in Colorado, I read that in addition to the essential cleanup of bloodstains and bullet holes, "The outdoor stairway around which two students died and five were injured has been rebuilt, widened and landscaped with terraces. As for the library, the scene of most of the carnage, it no longer officially exists. Workmen gutted the area and then sealed the entryway with a wall and two rows of blue lockers."[54] The terrible reality of what happened there has been covered over. I can think of no better way to insure that those who lived through it will be plagued forever with the evidence of their experience expressed in nightmares, anxiety, depression, and festering rage.

In a similar vein, I do not believe that cleansing the world of guns is a psychologically valid response to mass shootings. Personally, I do not know how to handle guns and am afraid of them, but the intensity of controversy around the subject of gun control tells me that firearms serve an important psychological function for many responsible men and women who *do* know how to handle them. The issue is not simple, but I suspect that in the long run, the consequences of leaving that part of the psyche unsatisfied could be worse than the harm done by guns. For the irresponsible few hell-bent on destruction, many instruments of death are readily available: small ones like garden tools and kitchen knives, and also extremely large ones—automobiles, fire, homemade bombs, airliners, and a whole raft of chemical and biological horrors that the criminal imagination can easily devise and may actually be more likely to in the event that conventional firearms are not at hand.

Fireworks, on the other hand, are a relatively harmless way for children and young people to experience the positive and negative potentials of explosives and learn how to handle them responsibly. Overly impressed by their dangers, however, the city council in my home town passed an ordinance banning personal fireworks. That year July Fourth came and went quietly, with none of the injuries or small brush fires that used to keep doctors and the fire department busy on Independence Day. One month later, however, the town had its worst fire in a century when a beloved historic building burned to the ground. Among the businesses lost was the oldest grocery store in Washington State, which also served as an informal community gathering place. No one died, but hardly a soul was unaffected by the fire, started in the night by two or three teenagers playing with matches. Earlier in the evening, the same youngsters had been seen setting off illegal fireworks.

Is there a connection between this tragedy and the fireworks ban? It would be hard to demonstrate a direct link, but the coincidence is highly suggestive. The explosive side of the psyche cannot be legislated out of existence, and the attempt to do so may actually make it more dangerous.

Nearly all my patients have violence-related problems, but the issues are quite different from what you might expect. My practice is not in what we would identify as poverty areas; on the contrary, it attracts a microcosm of the intelligent, self-reflective part of the population that can afford to spend time and money on analysis. Most of my patients are enlightened, humanitarian, pleasant people, with political beliefs more or less to the left of center. Many come from traditional religious backgrounds. They may have abandoned childhood religious affiliations, but still they espouse optimistic ideals with a Christian, Buddhist, or New-Age flavor.

A large subgroup are opposed to violence on principle, and have no access to their own capacity for violent action. Idealism has so desensitized them to normal emotional triggers that they are cheerfully unconscious of their negative perceptions and reactions. People who suffer from this syndrome, which looks to me like an injury to the fight-flight mechanism, cannot become healthily angry, stand up for themselves effectively, or defend their boundaries in appropriate ways. This puts severe limits on their capacity to individuate. I spend a lot of time and energy trying to help them find out how *they* feel instead of fantasizing how someone else feels and fulfilling the other person's real or imagined wants or needs. I call them "golden retriever people."

During the 1990s, golden retrievers became extremely popular as pets, mirroring the cultural condition I have described, in which idealistic images block the perception or expression of normal anger. Typically, golden retrievers are wonderfully gentle creatures that nearly everyone likes to have around, but the aggressive instinct seems to have been bred out of them. They often lack vitality, and at worst they fail at one of a dog's most important tasks, protecting its master. I keep hearing stories about golden retrievers sitting and wagging their tails while the house is robbed, happily keeping the burglars company. I gather that these animals are virtually incapable of violence but the gentle nature for which they have been bred comes with a price tag: Recent research shows that they have a genetic predisposition to cancer, which one study found "takes the life of up to 63 per cent of golden retrievers."[55]

In my experience, owners of golden retrievers often become impatient with their pets, even contemptuous. It is as if the dog's inability to behave aggressively activates the master's aggressiveness toward the dog. This points up an intrinsic connection between innocence and violence, for people who are too innocent tend to attract violence. That is, unconsciousness of the human shadow invites abuse from those who will not or cannot curb their own destructiveness. This is a familiar dynamic to violent young gang members, who sometimes search for easy victims who, as they say, look "vic" (like a victim); i.e., they are too naïve to be appropriately wary or fight back when attacked.[56]

Jung points out that every virtue, when carried to an extreme, turns into its opposite.[57] So it is with the Christian virtues today. Carried too far, ideals like kindness, caring, and self-sacrifice become people-pleasing manipulations or passive-aggressive martyrdom. These manifestations of the Judeo-Christian archetype are frequently acted out in the form of the three compulsively interlocking roles of the rescue triangle: rescuer, persecutor, and victim, behaviors that concretize the actions of the Old-Testament God, who alternately rescued and persecuted His people, and the New-Testament Christ, who was both rescuing savior and persecuted victim.[58]

We forget that Jesus did not just say, "Love your neighbor," but "Love your neighbor as yourself." People who do more for others than they can legitimately afford to give away cannot help feeling deprived and victimized, with destructive consequences for everyone concerned. However, the admonition "don't be selfish" is such a deeply ingrained ideal that it virtually drops from the sky when people most need to take care of their own best interests. It also comes out of the mouths of family members and friends who stand to lose when someone upon whom they are leaning stops being neurotically self-sacrificing.

Popular culture generates many images of a link between violence and fanatical Christian ideals. Such films as *Breaking the Waves*, *The Apostle*, *The Other Side of Sunday*, *Jindabyne*, and *The Good Shepherd* express the sad truth that too concrete an *imitatio Christi*, too literal an emulation of the Buddha of compassion, runs so counter to human reality that it cannot but fail. I would go so far as to say that these idealized attitudes are responsible for much of the violence we see today, that *violence is the human spirit's protest against the enforcement of more goodness than it can stomach*. Sometimes the interplay between violence and compulsory virtue takes place entirely within a single individual. In that case, a person tries to be so much better than she is, suppressing all the negative emotions that do not fit the ideal, that eventually the negativity erupts. However, the unit is equally likely to be a group: a family, a town, a nation. In that case, one or a few individuals may act out the violence for the whole group, allowing everyone else to preserve an exemplary appearance.

The widespread repression of negative emotion to sustain the appearance of virtue has produced a high level of ambient rage in the North American psyche. This furious unconscious background is one of the underlying reasons for the violent behavior of children. Children's undeveloped egos leave them particularly vulnerable to possession by any archetype that is activated in the collective psyche. Experts quoted in the media attribute school violence like the shootings at Jonesboro, Arkansas, or Littleton, Colorado, to the youngsters' personal psychology or to external factors such as availability of guns, media violence, gangs, or rap music. However, these explanations rarely hold water in the individual case. An understanding of depth psychology generates more durable hypotheses. Consider, for instance, that at least one of the young Jonesboro murderers was identified with fundamentalist Christian ideals that encourage projection of evil on others, and that the whole town was immersed in these ideals. It was a perfect setup for an eruption of the dark side of the God-image, the aspect of the Self that incarnates in criminal violence. Similarly, Littleton appears to be one of those beautifully manicured, perfect-appearing suburban neighborhoods. As for the United States as a whole, our culture's naïve idealism on the conscious side, accompanied by a high level of ambient rage in the unconscious, has created a dangerously incendiary state of affairs.

We are rarely aware of the ambient level of emotion because we are *in* it. It is like the air we breathe. We are profoundly affected, however, whether or not we perceive the unconscious background. The most sensitive and psychologically permeable people are the ones most affected. So are the weakest, least developed, and least stable. Like so many volunteer garbage collectors, the most gifted and the most damaged among us pick up whatever is activated in the collective psyche. If what they find is rage, they may become irrationally enraged; and if they lack the strength to contain and integrate such intense emotion, they may begin killing people at random.

On the other hand, this sort of explosiveness can be what fuels a creative person's productivity. Daniel, a sensitive and gifted inventor, had the following dream:

> A man tells me he has some leftover black powder and asks if I can use it. I say yes. Later I look out my window and can't believe my eyes. The gunpowder is arriving by dump truck, two full truckloads of it! I thought I had only agreed to take a little bit. I worry about the potential for harm in all this material, but I conclude that it will be all right as long as I keep it where it is, in my own back yard.
>
> I don't know how I'm going to use it all. Sifting through it, I discover that some is in the form of cakes with holes in them. These will have to be broken down into powder before they can be used.

The cakes with holes reminded Daniel of an ancient Stone Age tool used to straighten out bent spears. It is as if the destructive material contains the potential for its own transformation, the means to convert perverse (bent) instruments of violence into something useful. However, to avoid doing harm, he must keep the stuff in his own yard. In outer reality, Daniel vents anger freely in solitude (in his own yard) but is careful not to take his rage out on others. He harbors an immensely fertile creative life, which allows energies that could explode destructively to find benevolent outlets.

Some literature and art, of the sort that Jung called visionary, is like a collective dream, laying bare the archetypal underpinnings of a particular time and place. Don DeLillo's novel *Underworld*,[59] published in 1997, is such a work, one that affords an extraordinary overview of the problem of violence in the North American psyche during the last half of the Twentieth Century.

*Underworld* begins with the famous 1951 baseball game between the Brooklyn Dodgers and the New York Giants. The Giants win the game with a home run referred to as "the shot heard 'round the world." The phrase could equally well apply to an atomic explosion, and in fact the novel then segues into an underground nuclear test in the Soviet Union.

A sixteen-year-old from the Bronx named Nick Shay listens to the ballgame alone, rooting for the losing team. Nick is like an Everyman for the second half of the Twentieth Century, a collective ego, so to speak, embodying the development of the American consciousness from the first atomic bomb until today. At the age of seventeen, he picks up a sawed-off shotgun and more or less accidentally kills a man, mirroring our naive collective adolescent destructiveness when we first used the Bomb.

Nick serves a little time in detention and is then sent to a Jesuit school for rehabilitation. He (we North Americans) gradually repudiates his violent past and takes up a respectable life in

Phoenix, Arizona, where later, in the 1990s, he lives an anonymous life drinking soy milk, running marathons, and conscientiously recycling his trash. This innocuous, golden-retriever way of life reads like unconscious atonement for the collective guilt we all carry for the destruction of Hiroshima and Nagasaki. Nick is, after all, an executive in a toxic waste disposal company that cleans up radioactive trash just as, on a psychological level, certain people take care of the archetypal *shadow* for all of us, some by integrating it, others by acting it out.

As if to underscore the idea that someone is enacting the psyche's repressed violence, media announcements that the Texas freeway killer has shot another victim provide a ghostly background theme recurring throughout the novel.

As the century winds down and Nick reaches retirement age, he confides to the reader:

> I long for the days of disorder. I want them back, the days when I was alive on the earth, rippling in the quick of my skin, heedless and real. I was dumb-muscled and angry and real. This is what I long for, the breach of peace, the days of disarray when I walked real streets and did things slap-bang and felt angry and ready all the time, a danger to others and a distant mystery to myself.[60]

This electrifying confession of Nick's longing for his violent past is like the lament of a man who yearns for a connection to God. The over-civilized, overly corrected North American psyche hungers for something vital and real. When there is no connection with the Self, the wild, rebellious adolescent soul emits lethal energy that is periodically picked up and translated into criminal violence: an accidental shooting; a freeway killing; an outburst of deadly violence in the schools; a massive attack on our very way of life. It is hard to admit that, as terrible as were the events of September 11, they were also enlivening, giving impetus to a vitality, generosity, and heroism that represents the very best of the American psyche.

Perhaps it is no coincidence that, like Nick Shay, I had a dangerous, mid-century encounter with violence in late adolescence. Hanging around after hours in the high-school chemistry laboratory, I was gripped by an irrational impulse to carry a tiny piece of sodium across the room with a pair of laboratory tweezers, and drop it into a sink full of water. There was a flash of light and a terrifying burst of flame, a micro nuclear blast. I was luckier than Nick, for my teacher ran in from the next room to help contain the fire.

I was aware that sodium ignites in water, but had no idea how violent the reaction would be. It was as if some purposeful agent wanted me to find out. Nick Shay's not-so-accidental accident at the same age emerged from a similar state of knowing but not knowing. My son did something comparable in late adolescence when he picked and ate a poisonous but fortunately not lethal mushroom growing beside the road. Could it be that the adolescent psyche, on the eve of leaving home, is programmed for a dangerous and fateful encounter with the vitality and violence of the Self? Without it, perhaps the fledgling human never really leaves the nest.

In the wake of shooting sprees by those two preadolescent boys in Jonesboro, one of my patients asked me what I thought was behind this kind of crime. "If you really want to know," I said, "I think we are trying to make the world too safe for our children—safer than the psyche can bear."

Others have made similar observations. A mental health counselor who works with violent children brought into a hospital emergency room told me:

"I thought these violent kids would be from families that don't set enough limits, but it's often just the opposite. Of course some violent children have no supervision at all, but most of the ones I see are from incredibly restrictive, overly-controlled environments."

A woman who works with juvenile offenders in the Washington state prison system concurs.

For half a century or more, North Americans have been caught up in a mass effort to prevent anything bad from ever happening to anyone, and now we are seeing the disastrous consequences. I am quite sure that the violence of children—and also of the adults they become—will continue to escalate until we can accept the fact that the terrible side of life is here to stay; until we stop shielding kids from the normal, everyday kinds of pain, deprivation, and failure without which they cannot learn that their actions have consequences; until we understand that our Rhino nature is essential to psychological health and even physical survival.

Children need a certain amount of protection, to be sure, but our obsession with security has gone so far that its opposite now bursts out in outrageous acts. Children need adventure and risk. How else can they learn courage? They need legitimate challenges, ways to discover their limits, small hurts to stop them before they go too far. Telling them what not to do is not enough. They need to act independently, to experiment, to bump against the real consequences of real actions and meet the real darkness in life. Otherwise, how can they possibly grow into responsible adults?

Derek, obsessed with financial security and keeping his children safe, dreamed that he was trying to buy insurance but found out that it cost too much. Outside the dream, the job he hated but was afraid to leave was the symbolic insurance that made it possible to buy all the actual policies he carried: medical, disability, life, earthquake, fire, professional liability, collision, you name it. The premium that he and his family paid for all that security took the form of his periodic outbursts of rage. Collectively, our over-concern with safety is as costly as Derek's, and one of the ways we pay is in the violence of children.

If you think I am overstating the case, consider that one city's response to new guidelines for safety in public play areas was to remove the swings from its parks. The federal government prescribed a soft material covering the ground for a large area around swings to prevent injury if a child should fall. The city could not afford to do this and the cost of liability insurance became prohibitive. Then swings that had been safe enough for decades were taken down, not for the sake of the children but to avoid the risk of lawsuits.

Middle- and upper-class parents chauffeur their children everywhere in an effort to keep them safe, rarely allowing them to be alone, unscheduled, or unsupervised even in small rural communities. Most parents oversee their children's homework, and some *do it* for them to keep them from making mistakes. Laws controlling traffic around school buses, school zones, and crosswalks effectively train youngsters to walk into the street without looking, confident that vehicles will stop for them. Rather than trying to teach good judgment, we censor the books, movies, and television to which children are exposed. Parents bail their children out of every little difficulty, feeding the kids' belief that they should not have to suffer the consequences of what they do.

Prevailing approaches to psychotherapy aggravate the problem. When a person engages in violent or merely unusual behavior, therapists rarely look for the reason. They just try to make the problem go away, not understanding that symptoms are important communications. Drugs that eliminate symptoms without dealing with underlying causes effectively disable the psyche's self-healing processes. Such medications are increasingly the treatment of choice.

In my community, a twelve-year-old was arrested for setting a fire in a restaurant and the judge issued a strong warning that he should not play with matches. A few weeks later, when he pushed another student, the boy was suspended from school. A counselor dismissed him after a few sessions because he refused to talk about his fascination with fire. His mother felt helpless to deal with him and took him to a physician, hoping to have him medicated. Instead, the doctor wisely told the mother, "We have to keep talking to Raymond until we find out why he's doing this," but it was too late. The following week, while he and other children were playing on a barge, a friend dared him to drop a lighted match through an access hatch into a hull full of volatile fumes. The barge exploded, injuring six children.

Raymond was convicted of first-degree arson and six counts of reckless endangerment. Will prison teach him to handle fire responsibly? I do not think so. Perhaps, like many violent criminals, Raymond has brain damage, or maybe he is a hopeless psychopath. More likely, he is just a hormone-driven kid, desperate to ignite the vital spark within and leave dependency behind, a young man not so different from the ones who got this nation going in 1773 by dumping three-hundred forty-two chests of British tea into Boston Harbor.

What to do? We need to stop compulsively trying to create a world in which terrible things do not happen, accept the hard reality that they always will, and cultivate the courage to take some chances. I do not mean being foolish. I mean putting the swings back up, liability be damned. I mean letting our kids do their own homework, even if they do it wrong. I mean teaching them how to deal with likely dangers and sending them to school by themselves. I mean showing them how to shoot off fireworks without hurting themselves or starting fires. I mean finding ways to handle youngsters who bully their classmates without immediately removing them from school or society, which only increases the isolation they already feel. One thing on which the research agrees is that painful feelings of isolation are a precursor of child violence.[61]

To limit the worst kinds of violence we have to figure out what will satisfy the psyche's violent side without causing too much harm. Anger and rage need to be expressed. Imaginal expression is especially valuable, for violent and vengeful fantasies, in contrast to violent actions, hurt no one. Such fantasies are the healthy psyche's way of restoring a sense of dignity and self-respect when a person has been discounted, shunned, or actively abused.

A 1971 field study[62] found that, contrary to the conventional wisdom, watching fantasy-violence on television *reduced* the destructive acting-out of some groups of adolescent and pre-adolescent boys. Subsequent research has shown that the effect depends partly on the child's age, his socioeconomic status, and how much he identifies with the televised perpetrator, but the basic result remains. More than three decades later there is still little if any public recognition that media violence can have redeeming social value. Findings at odds with the prevailing belief that violent images provoke violent actions are simply overlooked.

Violent images are in our face today because we need them. They do not cause violence, but are symptomatic of the stressfulness of contemporary life, which creates an enormous need for fantasy outlets for anger and rage. A young man says, "When the world pisses you off and you need a place to vent, [the video game] *Quake* is a great place for it. You can kill somebody and watch the blood run down the walls, and it feels good. But when it's done, you're rid of it."[63] I think he knows what he is talking about.

Cultural forms of imaginal violence have provided catharsis for the troubled soul since at least as far back as the Greek tragedies, the earliest myths and fairy tales, and—yes—the Bible. In today's world, various forms of art including movies serve the same function. As film director Julie Taymor puts it, "We [artists] will never deny our fascination with violence. It's part of telling stories, it's part of being artists and always has been. We need art to exorcize our demons. That's our job, that was Shakespeare's job—to put out there what is real but unspoken, so it can be released and understood."[64]

Taymor's appallingly violent film *Titus*, a version of Shakespeare's "Titus Andronicus," is one of my favorites. So are many others, among them *Dr. Strangelove, Blue Velvet, The Silence of the Lambs, The Crying Game, Pulp Fiction, Fargo*, the New York *Hamlet, In the Bedroom, Mystic River, Crash, Babel, The Wind that Shakes the Barley, Letters from Iwo Jima, The Lives of Others*, and *Michael Clayton*. The vitality and authenticity of such productions make a mockery of more saccharine slices of movie life, yet many people refuse to see films with violent content. For some it is a matter of principle, for others, aversion. To many of my friends, I imagine my interest in violence may seem a little off-color or worse, for violence is numinous to me. I suspect it is numinous to others as well, especially people who cannot or will not look at it. Violence occupies the place in today's psyche that sex had early in the *last* century, fascinating but utterly taboo.

The idealistic attitudes behind the refusal to look at violent images create intense, even violent, opposition to the most valuable tools we have for gaining access to the value and meaning inherent in angry emotions. In addition to violent stories, movies, and other works of art, there are war games, video games, fireworks, toy guns, and real firearms. All these things can be used to redeem the psyche trapped in dark fantasies and bring order into chaotic emotional states.

Rituals, including target shooting and hunting, are one of the most effective ways we have to express and contain violent energy. I especially like rituals that develop spontaneously from the individual imagination, but there are collective ones as well, such as football games and the increasingly popular extreme sports.

People need this sort of activity to get an accurate sense of their own power in relation to the power of others. Sometimes the word *power* is pronounced with a sideways glance and slightly lowered voice, as if it were a dirty word, but power is one of the psyche's great ruling principles and we overlook it at our peril. The Christian era has taught us too little about how to carry worldly power in non-destructive ways because Jesus separated himself decisively from it, saying, "Get thee behind me, Satan." However, whether power works for good or evil depends entirely on what is done with it. Like guns, dynamite, or nuclear energy, its effect depends on the consciousness of the person who has it, on whether he knows how to use it responsibly or is merely possessed by the raw, unrestrained archetype, which gobbles up power for its own sake and uses it to dominate or violate others.

The word *power* derives from a root that means "to be able," and is defined as "The ability or capacity to act or perform effectively." Humans need to assert themselves, to exercise their competence, and above all, to protect themselves from violation by others.

At bottom, the rage that leads to violent action is a natural, instinctive response to a real or imagined threat to the core sense of individual identity carried by the Self. *Some—maybe all—destructively violent actions spring from the ego's inability to respect, confront, and wrestle with the Self's enraged response to galling levels of powerlessness.* I suspect that the only real solution to out-of-control violence will come through the responsible exercise of power in the service of the Self.

If I were the therapist of Raymond the firebug I would give him as much power as he can learn to carry responsibly. I would give him a full box of kitchen matches and watch him light them, one by one, let them burn down, and drop them into a bowl of water. I would help him light and observe the effects of fires in many different contexts: bonfires, cooking fires, and fireworks; fires in fireplaces and clearings in the woods; even spectacular chemical fires created by the combustion of sodium in water. I would require him to sit through the movie *Bambi*, with its horrifying scene of animals fleeing from an advancing forest fire. I would give him a waterproof box in which to carry his own supply of matches, and even show him how to start a fire without them.

Naive? Foolish? Innocence of the sort that invites violence? I do not think so. A condition of Raymond's probation after he started the restaurant fire was that he stay away from matches. That only escalated the problem, and as I said before, talk-therapy did not work. I like to think I would dare try something different, risking lawsuits and my professional reputation by getting Raymond really close to the awesome faces of fire and showing him how to handle it. I like to think I would take a chance on making the world less safe.

CHAPTER SIX

# Sedating the Savage

"Swallowed half an hour before closing time, that second dose of soma had raised a quite impenetrable wall between the actual universe and their minds. Bottled, they crossed the street; bottled, they took the lift up to Henry's room."

—ALDOUS HUXLEY[65]

I am hardly the first to note the irony of North America's so-called "war on drugs." We are a drug-addicted culture, through and through, with chemical solutions for every discomfort. We rush to sedate the pain of body and soul, suppressing symptoms that, as often as not, embody the endangered Rhino voice within us, crying out in savage protest against some aspect of how we are living.

Substances to which we are expected to "just say no" comprise an arbitrary few of the toxic, often addictive, mind-altering chemicals at our disposal. Psychoactive prescription drugs are the worst. I am appalled to hear that the antidepressant Paxil has been pushed on national television as a cure for shyness, as if shyness were a disease! God help those of us who are naturally introverted in aggressively extraverted societies such as ours that have the will and the ability to annihilate the diffident, inner-centered nature of a large portion of humanity.

Paxil is one of a cornucopia of seductive chemicals that promise to cookie-cut us into ever more limited and idealized images of emotional well-being. Vacuous smiles are gradually replacing the interesting and varied facial expressions of my friends, relatives, and even the street people in my hometown. In my dark imaginings, mental health professionals are rounding up the homeless in the dead of night, handing out free samples of happiness pills. The fixed smiles of pharmacological good feeling disturb me more than I can say. They do not bespeak authentic joy or contentment, only blunted responsiveness.

Behind our multiple dependencies on prescription drugs, over-the-counter analgesics, cold remedies, alcohol, nicotine, caffeine and street drugs lies something more insidious: the addiction to feeling good. North Americans harbor the assumption, rarely examined, that an ill-defined condition called happiness is the only proper state of mind, and that a person is entitled—even required—to feel good no matter what.

In view of the rampant use of happiness medications, it should be no surprise that Ecstasy is one of today's common street drugs. Called the "hug drug," it is said to produce euphoria, empathy, and delicious sensuality. Ecstasy is popular in spite of unresolved questions about long-term brain damage. Similarly, the demand for psychotropics is barely affected by evidence that extended use may have deleterious consequences.

Chemical happiness was not so easy to come by in the nineteen-thirties and forties when I was a child. When my father became severely depressed, he had no choice but to suffer. He frequently sat at the breakfast table with tears rolling down his face. I never dared ask what was the matter and no one else did either, so his problems were never explored. Then, in the late nineteen-fifties, the first minor tranquilizer was synthesized and the family doctor put my father on Miltown. The drug suppressed the symptoms enough to convince the doctor and perhaps also my father that he was happier. At least he caused the rest of us less distress. However, his artificial tranquility often allowed him to drive serenely down the wrong side of the road, undisturbed by thoughts of possible danger. It is one of life's small miracles that no one was killed or maimed. Eventually he happily exposed himself sexually to a pre-adolescent boy, a trauma of no small proportions for the youngster, my mother, and not least my father who, in the confusion of his medicated state, was never quite sure whether or not he actually did what the boy said.

I imagine he did. I believe the drug blocked healthy inhibitions that had, until then, kept him from acting out his pedophilic impulses. He lived the last years of his life in a swampland of demented fantasies, his psyche's last desperate attempt to be heard in spite of the drug's power to suppress it. If anyone had encouraged him to reflect upon the symptoms of his underlying problems—his sorrows, fantasies, frustrations, and rage—he might have found his way into a more authentic and productive life. Driven underground, the inner protest merely grew larger and more primitive until it overwhelmed him.

Today, psychoactive drugs are routinely used to support the happiness myth, to enforce perfectionist, constricted, idealistic values that are out of touch with dark psychological realities. Although legitimate applications of such medications exist, they are rare. Occasionally a well-chosen psychotropic can be useful to contain severe symptoms long enough to permit an otherwise disabled person to engage a therapeutic process, preferably in small doses and for a short time. For instance, my former patient Tim told me that his family doctor prescribed Lorazapam (Valium) to relieve his fear of flying. He writes:

> I have taken it several times. I flew to L.A. last year with my wife and Lorazapam—my first flight in ten years. Last summer I flew to San Francisco alone with Lorazapam. Then, a few weeks ago, my wife and I flew to L.A. and San Diego and I took nothing. My overall experience with the drug was that it showed me where I was capable of going myself. [I found out that I] *can* feel very low and cool and quiet. I didn't know there was such an internal lowness and coolness and quietness available to me. Lorazapam showed me that there was. I am now better at getting there myself.

Psychotropics should only be employed the way Tim did, with caution and as a means to the end of authentic psychological healing. Instead, they are too often imagined to be a cure in themselves and are used indiscriminately. They function to allay fears of deviance—a.k.a. eccentricity or individuality—calming the anxieties of parents, friends, relatives, and doctors who cannot tolerate the pain and unusual behaviors that are part of any deep healing process. The part of a person that is like The Rhino is put to sleep, and healing remains dangerously shallow.

I did not realize how far we had gone down the road toward enforced uniformity until a few years ago, when I consulted an internist about an interference with my breathing that was waking me at night. It was a minor medical problem, later solved quickly and simply by an ear, nose and throat specialist, but the internist, whom I'll call Dr. Wright, nearly turned it into a catastrophe.

Disregarding my communication that I react strongly to drugs and need to start with small doses of any medication, he prescribed large doses of an inhalant that has anxiety as its primary side effect.

Thanks to the drug, the next time I went to Dr. Wright's office I was extremely anxious, and he jumped to the conclusion that I was having a panic attack. In a remarkable demonstration of circular reasoning, he then concluded that panic attacks were responsible for the breathing problem for which I had originally consulted him. Therefore, he concluded, I should take Xanax, a potent psychoactive chemical. I politely refused. He wrote out a prescription and placed it in my hand. I walked out of his office and he followed me through a crowded waiting room, begging me to take the medicine.

At the door I turned to him and said, "Give me a break. I'm not a dummy."

A young woman among the audience of curious patients giggled.

"You give *me* a break," he said. "Patients have to *trust* their doctors."

I keep the unfilled prescription in my files to remind me never to indulge in blind trust. My son tells me that Xanax is addictive and is prized on the street for its mind-altering properties. When it is used medically, insomnia and dizziness are common side effects. Because it depresses the central nervous system, patients are warned to avoid activities that require mental alertness. When the drug is withdrawn, a rebound effect often produces anxiety more severe that the original symptom.

Another physician told me that Xanax would certainly make it impossible to do my work. This reminded me that I had not been able to function professionally for the better part of a day because of the cognitive side effects of a single dose of yet another medication that Dr. Wright once prescribed—something I later learned was in any case the wrong drug for the problem he imagined it would help.

An incompetent doctor? Yes. Yet Dr. Wright had a full practice of apparently satisfied patients. His efforts to coerce me to take Xanax were only an extreme variant of the many ways in which mind-altering drugs are pushed by practitioners in every city and town in this country, otherwise competent doctors who have little or no knowledge of the psyche.

I was lucky. As a psychologist I had the expertise to know that I was not having panic attacks, and that I would not choose to medicate them if I were. Because I make a point of reading package inserts, I knew that anxiety is a common side effect of the inhalant Dr. Wright prescribed. More important, I understand the value of anxiety. My emotional reactions told me that Dr. Wright was a danger to me. Listening to this primal inner voice enabled me to get away from the doctor before he caused me irreparable harm.

Not everyone is so fortunate. Every few weeks I hear of another abuse of psychoactive medication by a general practitioner or even a psychiatrist. A man in the midst of a prolonged and potentially fruitful introversion is put on antidepressants. So is a woman grieving, as she must, the loss of her only son. A boy who fidgets in school and sasses the teacher because he is bored is given Ritalin. A young woman receiving healing messages from God is hospitalized and injected with antipsychotic medication. A woman with a slowly growing brain tumor is given an antidepressant that masks her symptoms, delaying detection of the tumor. These are not isolated incidents. They have become the norm.

A friend whose aged father has been wrestling with cancer writes:

> My father is now recovering nicely after many worrisome returns to the hospital. You might be interested to know that the culprit to his near downfall was not his cancer but overmedication by a psychiatrist. I had been telling them to take him off Depakote [an anti-seizure drug also sometimes prescribed to relieve manic symptoms] since before his surgery, but it took them three months and three additional trips to the hospital (mostly emergency for vertigo and extreme weakness) to finally come to this conclusion themselves. He is now off that dreaded drug and most others and doing better.

Not long after my encounter with Dr. Wright, an acquaintance asked my advice about his adolescent daughter. Jenny had been depressed for several years and had been, he said, a "difficult child" all her life. What would I think about putting her on Prozac?

I knew the family well enough to suspect that there were good reasons for Jenny's unhappiness, and I thought that giving her Prozac would only be an attempt to control her. I told her father that it is fashionable to think of depression as a disease, but that I see it differently.

"In my experience," I said, "there are usually reasons why a person is depressed—reasons that aren't necessarily obvious. If Jenny were my child I'd want to find out what's going on. Why don't you send her to a good therapist?"

Several weeks later I met him on the street. "How's Jenny?" I asked.

"She's mending beautifully."

"Mending? Is she sick?"

"Didn't I tell you? She broke her neck."

"My God! How did that happen?"

"She dove into the shallow end of the pool. The doctor says she's doing magnificently, though. She'll be fine."

Wondering if my recommendation had somehow led to Jenny's injury, I asked what he had done about her depression.

"Hey," he said, "She's on Prozac. It's fantastic. She's a different person. So much easier to get along with. Before, it was like having a black cloud in the house. Now . . ."

A shadow flickered across his face. He looked away and said quickly, "Of course, without the Prozac she might not have had the accident, but . . ."

Then, as if the disquieting idea had not interrupted his train of thought, he went on enthusiastically reporting the benefits of the drug.

The particulars of Jenny's accident can be read symbolically, like a dream. Diving into the pool would be like diving into her own psyche, but instead of exploring the unconscious depths of her depression, she was given the shallow solution offered by a drug, which served to break the connection between her consciousness—her head—and the emotional realities lodged in her body. Jenny is an experienced swimmer and diver. She knew that what she did was dangerous, but Prozac disconnected her from the emotional warning system that would have prevented her foolish action. Like nothing so much as the happiness drug soma in Aldous Huxley's *Brave New World*, Prozac "raised a quite impenetrable wall between the actual universe and [her mind]."

In 1932, when Huxley's classic science fiction novel was first published, everyone understood that the world he described was a chilling dystopia. Young people reading the book today, however, are apt to miss the point because so much of what the book describes has actually come to pass. Huxley set his story six-hundred years in the future, but in the foreword to the 1946 second edition he wrote that things were progressing faster than expected. "Today it seems quite possible," he said, "that the horror may be upon us within a single century."[66] Even at that he underestimated the speed of change. In the early Twenty-First Century, our cultural ideals are so shockingly similar to what Huxley called a horror that the words "brave new world" have lost the irony they once carried in everyday speech. Not too many years ago a newspaper headline exulted, "Nasdaq tops 5000: Record ushers in a brave new world!" while elected officials solemnly congratulated themselves upon "our brave new world."

The society Huxley created is a totalitarian one whose members are, as he put it, "a population of slaves who do not have to be coerced because they love their servitude."[67] Happiness is valued as the highest good and, thanks to the psychoactive drug soma, no one has to suffer any strong emotions. In fact emotions are not permitted. In the unlikely event that someone refuses to swallow the daily ration of happiness pills, he or she is gently but firmly persuaded.

Long before the advent of Muzak, Huxley conceived a Synthetic Music Box incessantly piping The Voice of Reason and the Voice of Good Feeling into the environment while genetic engineering and factory incubation eliminate troublesome individual differences by making perfectly uniform and identical babies.

As one of the characters puts it, "The world's stable now. People are happy; they get what they want, and they never want what they can't get. They're well off; they're safe; they're never ill . . . And if anything should go wrong, there's soma."[68]

115

When *Brave New World* was written, the actual synthesis of artificial, mind-altering drugs was still in the future. Preparations of opium extracted from poppies, particularly a tincture called laudanum, were the tranquilizers of choice. In the United States, alcoholic beverages were illegal and there were increasing efforts to control the use of opium. Prefrontal lobotomy was first used to manage psychosis in 1935,[69] three years after Huxley published his novel. The anti-psychotic drug chlorpromazine would not be synthesized for another two decades. Then, in 1955, Wallace Laboratories made Miltown, the first minor tranquilizer. They also produced a muscle relaxant they had the temerity to call Soma! Librium entered the marketplace in 1960, Valium in 1963. Thereafter, varieties of psychoactive medication burgeoned.

The word "tranquilizer" first appeared in the lay press in 1955. Six years later, Alice Glaser used it in a science-fiction short story "The Tunnel Ahead,"[70] in which tranquilizers provide a way to subdue emotional reactions to the stresses of extreme overpopulation. The members of a young family of five, returning to New York in bumper-to-bumper traffic after a day at the beach, are shoehorned into a regulation-tiny car much as airline passengers are today. The direct effects of the crowding described are nearly unbearable, especially for the children, but gradually the reader becomes aware of an even greater source of anxiety, a nameless dread attached to a tunnel through which every vehicle returning to the city must pass. Only after the family barely makes it through is the reason for the escalating tension revealed: This society controls its mushrooming population by closing the tunnel at random intervals and euthanizing everyone who happens to be inside.

In reality, the anxiety born of overcrowding would probably motivate a search for solutions, such as the development of adequate birth control. In the story, however, the functions of anxiety have been disabled. A pop-out drawer containing tranquilizers is standard equipment on every car. The pills are used liberally for the purpose that Ritalin often is today, to keep people from rebelling against conditions that are intolerable, especially for normally active children.

As I write, National Public Radio[71] tells of a study that has documented large increases in the number of prescriptions written for Ritalin, antidepressants, and Clonadine for children between the ages of two and four. These medications, frequently given very young children to enable them to meet the requirements of preschool, are prescribed despite the absence of information about their effects on the immature, developing brain, and in the face of package inserts specifying that Ritalin is not appropriate for children under six, nor Clonadine under twelve.

Roxanne was nearly expelled from preschool at the age of three because of disruptive actions such as throwing chairs. Her mother had no idea why she was so aggressive and impulsive. The little girl was diagnosed with attention deficit hyperactivity disorder and put on Ritalin. She calmed down and was able to stay in preschool. Now she has been on the drug for seven years; and incidentally, her development is so delayed that only now, at the age of ten, has she begun to read. The crucial question was not addressed: Was a developmental disorder the cause of Roxanne's disruptive behavior, or was it the Ritalin itself that interrupted her development?

In an article about the extent to which our culture suppresses healthy masculinity, George W. S. Trow comments on the use of psychotropics with somewhat older children:

I read . . . that between ten and twelve per cent of American male children between the ages of six and fourteen are on Ritalin. It calms them down, it clams them up; it makes them controllable; it overcomes some of the symptoms, at least, of attention-deficit disorder. It must be annoying—or maddening—to these naturally active, curious, aggressive young males to understand intuitively (as they surely must do—watching *Animal House*, say, or *Natural Born Killers*, or *Pulp Fiction*) that they are being drugged out of the mind-set of the culture they are in natural reaction to.[72]

In 1999 it was reported that at least a million prescriptions for antidepressants were being written for teens and prepubescent children in the United States every year, and even more youngsters—as many as five per cent—were diagnosed yearly as clinically depressed.[73] In the first decade of the Twenty-First Century these figures continue to grow. Consider the implications: Taking account of only two of the most popular diagnoses—depression and attention deficit disorder—our culture defines the emotional state of at least one out of every six adolescent and preadolescent children as sick and tries to medicate it out of existence. This suggests that either the way we are living is driving our children crazy, or that we are pathologizing large numbers of healthy children because they do not conform to our expectations. I suspect it is a little of each.

We seem to have forgotten that emotions are an important part of people. More often than not, a so-called negative emotion is a response to something that may need to change. I would not be surprised if today's high levels of anxiety, depression, and inability to concentrate were a natural consequence of the fast-paced, over-stimulating conditions of contemporary life. By damping down our authentic reactions, psychoactive medications allow us to keep trying to conform to feel-good expectations that are severely out of line with human reality. Like the science-fictional societies imagined by Huxley and Glaser, we are in extreme denial, repressing so much of our inner world that we feel as if mind-altering drugs are the only way to keep the resulting internal pressures under control. If drugs were not so available, cultural conditions would have to change to accommodate the way people are, rather than the other way around.

In 1961, the year that "The Tunnel Ahead" was published, several studies demonstrated that the active ingredient in Librium and Valium is remarkably effective in taming animals. This drug was found to abolish the fighting response in mice, monkeys, tigers, lions, dingo dogs, and squirrels. In other words, tranquilizers subdue fight-flight reactions which, though unpleasant, may be essential to survival. Agreeable compliance is not the appropriate response to every situation, and when the instinctive, Rhino level of the psyche has not been tranquilized it tells us when to fight back.

Too few contemporary practitioners of the healing arts realize that such disagreeable emotions as rage, sorrow, and fear are necessary parts of the human equipment, and that to amputate a symptom without understanding its underlying purpose can have serious, even fatal, consequences. The trouble is, finding out what is behind a symptom is difficult and time-consuming, and healing may ultimately require major life changes. Many patients prefer the deceptively simple expedient of a pill, especially when they do not fully understand that there may be better options. Moreover, most insurance companies, eager for immediate results, will pay for medication but not psychotherapy, despite growing evidence that the results of even short-term psychotherapy are more permanent than those produced by drugs, making therapy the more economical long-range choice.[74]

The training of psychotherapists is so dominated by the cultural bias that even patients who want to know themselves more deeply have trouble finding practitioners equipped to guide them. These are the people described by Joan Acocella as seeking "a chance for a serious life,"[75] or in the words of T. M. Luhrman, "a sense of human complexity, of depth, an exigent demand to struggle against one's own refusals, and a respect for the difficulty of human life."[76] Ironically, the ancient alchemists, who can be seen as the first depth psychologists, knew more about the ingredients of psychological integration than many contemporary therapists. The old magical-sounding metaphorical recipes called for items like feces, urine, and vomit, and the first stage of the transformation process was named the *nigredo*—the blackness—because the alchemists correctly intuited that real healing only occurs when we turn inward and reflect upon the most repugnant parts of ourselves and the darkest, most miserable aspects of our lives.

If, as I believe, using drugs to limit human variation undermines the psyche's self-regulating and self-healing functions, we can expect the psyche to resist its own destruction with an eventual backlash. That is when the dark side of The Rhino bursts out. Drug-resistant lethal behaviors may develop in much the same way as, on the physical level, increasingly deadly drug-resistant bacteria have resulted from the overuse of antibiotics. A case in point may be the upsurge of violent crime among middle- and upper-class children that occurred in the 1990s at the same time as a big wave of enthusiasm for medicating children. It is intuitively obvious that the two things are connected, but the scientific question has yet to be answered: Is the apparent association between psychotropics and violence a coincidence or is there an actual cause-and-effect relationship? If the latter, which way does the causality go?

The truism that drugs and violence go together usually refers to illegal drugs and ghetto violence. However, there may also be a connection between prescription drugs and shootings in the schools. For instance, at least three of four boys who made headlines by shooting classmates, teachers, and parents between May of 1998 and May of 1999 were or had been on prescribed psychoactive drugs. Eric Harris, one of the boys who killed thirteen students and a teacher at Columbine High School in Colorado was taking the antidepressant Luvox; Thomas Solomon, who wounded six classmates in Conyers, Georgia, was on Ritalin; and Kipland Kinkel, who killed his parents and a student and wounded eight others in Springfield, Oregon, had first been given Ritalin and later Prozac.[77]

When two events such as violence and the use of drugs are correlated, we tend to assume a cause-and-effect relationship consistent with what we already believe, in this case that illegal drugs breed violence. We have images of shootouts between warring dealers and of deprived addicts stealing money to buy drugs. However, our faith in chemical cures for life's unpleasant realities biases us to believe that if someone on antidepressants commits a violent crime, then mental illness, not drugs, was behind the violence. We have faith that medicating disturbed people will reduce violence, even though this reverses the relationship between violence and illegal drugs. It also overlooks the fact that the youngsters just mentioned were already medicated when they started shooting. In short, we demonize street drugs as a primary cause of violence and simultaneously deify prescription drugs as a way to prevent violent acting out.

It is important to understand that the statistic of correlation expresses the extent to which two variables occur together, but does not provide information about causality.[78] If X and Y are correlated, X may be the cause of Y; Y the cause of X; or something else may be the cause of both. For instance, in the United States there is a high correlation between the annual sales of chewing gum and the incidence of crime, but prohibiting the sale of chewing gum would not be likely to reduce crime. The reason for the correlation is that both variables depend on the size of the population.

Similarly, without additional information, we can only speculate about the meaning of a correlation between drugs and violence. Once we have set aside the violence that arises from the lucrative business of peddling illegal substances, it makes no sense to apply different hypotheses to street drugs and prescription medications. Regardless of whether they are bought on the street or in a pharmacy, by definition, mind-altering drugs change a person's psychological functioning. Perhaps it is less self-evident that they may make permanent changes in the brain, but evidence of such effects is growing. At the end of the Twentieth Century, some twenty million people were taking Prozac, and symptoms referred to as "Prozac backlash" were already well documented. By then, several studies had found that about sixty per cent of people using SSRIs (selective serotonin reuptake inhibitors, the class of drug to which Prozac belongs) experience serious sexual dysfunction including decreased arousal and delayed orgasm. There were also many reports of motor disturbances of the sort that occur when there is a lesion in the brain, including tics, muscle spasms, and involuntary pelvic thrusting.[79]

Since that time, research has revealed direct evidence of structural changes in the brains of people taking SSRIs, an effect that has caused particular concern about what these drugs may do to the developing brains of children. Studies have also shown that depressed children and adolescents taking SSRIs are more likely to attempt both suicide and homicide than those given a placebo, research that is congruent with the high incidence of prescription drug use among the adolescent killers mentioned earlier. The evidence is alarming enough that in 2003 the British government sent a letter to health professionals saying that a review of the effectiveness of SSRIs indicated that their benefits did not outweigh their potential risks. Subsequently Britain banned the prescription of six of these drugs to children: Paxil, Zoloft, Effexor, Celexe, Lexapro, and Luvox. Strangely, Prozac escaped the ban.[80]

If the unpleasant emotions we are prone to associate with mental illness are, as I have suggested, essential aspects of the healthy psyche, exploring exactly how emotions serve us might help to explain a relationship between violence and psychoactive drugs. What if symptoms like depression and anxiety foster the kind of self-reflection that discourages impulsive destructiveness? If that is the case, using tranquilizers or antidepressants would prevent the necessary reflection. Or consider the possibility that certain prescription drugs, as well as some of the street variety, directly block inhibitions that normally keep people from translating lethal fantasies into action. If such an effect were to override the "taming" capacity of tranquilizers, violent acting-out would follow. Another possibility is that tranquilizers blur the distinction between fantasizing violence and actually committing a violent act. Fear of the consequences may be the only thing that keeps some people from taking literal vengeance on their enemies rather than merely fantasizing retribution. If that is so, then tranquilizing the fear of consequences would lead to violence.

Possibly, on the other hand, tranquilizers simply interfere with normal fantasy activity. Violent fantasies, in contrast to criminally violent actions, are the healthy psyche's way of working through the pain people feel when they are shunned, bullied, discounted, or otherwise mistreated. Research shows that at least some psychoactive drugs suppress dreaming, so it would not be surprising to find that they also interfere with the normal exercise of fantasy.

A substantial body of research supports the paradoxical conclusion that fear of fear is a primary cause of panic attacks:

> . . . some people consider anxiety symptoms—sweaty palms, a racing heart or shortness of breath—as harbingers of ill health, while others consider them simply as transient nuisances. People in the former group are more likely to panic under stress. . . . People with panic disorder are extremely anxiety-sensitive.[81]

In my practice I have noticed that fear of one's own rage often makes a person anxious, and I would venture to suggest that excessive fear of *any* emotion—anger, anxiety, fear, sorrow, even love—will tend to amplify it. Jung put it this way:

> If anything of importance is devalued in our conscious life, and perishes . . . there arises a compensation in the unconscious. We may see in this an analogy to the conservation of energy in the physical world, for our psychic processes also have a quantitative, energic aspect. No psychic value can dis-

appear without being replaced by another of equivalent intensity. This is a fundamental rule which is repeatedly verified in the daily practice of the psychotherapist and never fails.[82]

In other words, when we try to get rid of an important part of ourselves such as an unpleasant emotion, it does not disappear, but only becomes unconscious. Unseen or unacknowledged, it grows larger, more primitive, more insistent, and therefore more dangerous. However, if it is honored and given its due it may be the very thing that will bring healing.

The protagonist of *Brave New World* is named the Savage. He is a more civilized, humanized form of the energies in the psyche expressed by The Rhino. The Savage's inability to stomach a perfect world is expressed quite literally when, at one point, he goes behind a tree and vomits. Later he confesses, "I don't want comfort, I want God, I want poetry, I want real danger, I want freedom, I want goodness. I want sin. . . . I claim the right to be unhappy."[83]

The Savage in each of us can redeem us from the living hell of enforced happiness. As Jung wrote, "We must dig down to the primitive, and only from the conflict between civilized man and the . . . barbarian will there come what we need: a new experience of God."[84] Digging up the Savage is a dangerous enterprise, but current events sufficiently demonstrate that the wild one is upon us and will not be put off. Both children and adults will increasingly be compelled to act out the most brutal forms of violence until there are enough people who can and will consciously integrate and take responsibility for the part of themselves that is as violent as a rhinoceros, a task that psychoactive drugs can only abort.

Near the end of Huxley's novel, a man in a position of official responsibility reads a discourse written by the Savage. Drawn to the ideas in it, but aware that they represent a danger to the social order, he reflects that their author has the power to make people lose faith in the absolute value of happiness and cause them to believe "that the goal is somewhere beyond, somewhere outside the present human sphere; that the purpose of life is not the maintenance of well-being, but some intensification and refining of consciousness, some enlargement of knowledge."[85]

This is the power of the Savage in the human psyche. I like to think that it is stronger than the wish for happiness. I like to think that it is indestructible.

# CHAPTER SEVEN

# The End and the Beginning

"They asked Him, 'How shall we know the way to the King-
dom of Heaven?' and He commanded them, 'Follow the
birds, the beasts and the fishes and they will lead you in.'"

AN APOCRYPHAL GOSPEL[86]

O ne day, something of substance unexpectedly appears
among the catalogs and credit-card offers that clog my
mailbox. It is the first in a series of oddly interrelated
events. After a while, I begin to imagine that a giant hand is drop-
ping pebbles in front of me, as if some higher intelligence were
trying to steer me toward The Rhino and the natural world for
which he speaks. Then I see Pat Britt at a dinner party, and what
she tells me makes me wonder if I should be thinking in terms of
large, discrete raindrops instead of pebbles. Over blackberry-
cabernet sorbet, she suddenly recalls a dream she had the night
before about hanging out under the great world tree when a warm
rain begins to fall. She looks up and sees The Rhino draped over
a branch above her head. He is urinating.

I wonder if it is time to build an ark and begin loading animals and people, two by two. It is the wettest spring I have ever seen in Port Townsend, New England is beset with floods, last year New Orleans suffered Katrina, and the polar ice is melting. All things considered, the need for a latter-day Noah seems right in line with reality.

I drop the junk mail into my recycling bin and sit down at the fifty-year-old yellow pine dining table that serves as my writing desk. After a glance past the computer screen to see if any wildlife is emerging from the woods outside the window, I open the manila envelope whose return address, Wind Harvest Company, belongs to an old friend. Out of the blue, he has sent me a collection of essays concerning the vital role of wilderness in the psyche and in the world. He knows nothing about The Rhino, but I note that the book contains a piece by Laurens van der Post, "Appointment with a Rhinoceros," which I read on the spot. It describes the author's electrifying confrontation with an outer-world rhinoceros and the profound meaning this numinous encounter held for him:

> I had no doubt then that by opening our imagination to the beauty and diversity of . . . nature in Africa, nature would unlock a way towards a form of wholeness which we are compelled to find within ourselves if we are not to perish. It is a wholeness that surpasses and transcends all the paradoxical, contradictory and apparently conflicting necessities of life: a self wherein we see as in a mirror a bright reflection of the author of creation within and without. So that morning and through the days that followed, the rhinoceros walked at the head of a long procession of animals that seemed . . . to me pilgrims on an evolutionary journey of time that is a measure of the abiding and as yet unfinished business of creation.[87]

A few weeks later I am riveted by another unusual book that falls into my hands as if by accident. Jungian analyst Jerome Bernstein discusses what he calls Borderland consciousness, an emergent phenomenon of the psyche that defies our culture's over-confidence in the gods of science and rationality. Borderland people are perfectly sane individuals taken captive by non-rational experiences of the natural world, such as hearing animals talk to them or feeling the pain of injured trees in their own bodies. Various forms of environmental illness also belong to this realm. In recent years I, like Bernstein, have seen increasing numbers of people who fit this description. He theorizes that the development is part of "a 're-connection with nature' that is taking place in western culture." He says, "I am talking here of a profound, psychic process in which the very psychological nature and structure of the western ego is evolving through dramatic changes. It is becoming something more, and different from, what we have known in the past."[88] Pat Britt's relationship with both outer-world animals and The Rhino provided my first glimpse of what Bernstein is talking about.

The next event in the sequence is an inner one. It happens on a glorious spring morning while I am eating breakfast and watching the birds and animals that share my modest in-town acreage. A pregnant doe passes the window, followed closely by last year's offspring. Soon she will give birth to a tiny spotted fawn or two and send the yearlings away to fend for themselves. The birds are in various stages of nesting: goldfinches and rosy-colored house finches, white- and gold-crowned sparrows, pine siskins, grosbeaks, Stellers jays, red-winged blackbirds, robins, juncos, towhees, varied thrushes, downy woodpeckers, flickers and others whose names I do not know. This year they are all made cautious by the specter of a Cooper's hawk making its home nearby. A pair of gigantic crows have taken up residence in one of the tall firs behind my house, and the barn owl I saw one night at dusk may be there too.

During the twenty-three years that I have lived in this small community, escalating profits from land development have crowded out more and more of the local wildlife. Chances are that my friend the doe will find places to hide her babies in the tall grass that I keep in its natural, unmown state, but her options are quickly disappearing.[89] It still hurts to think about the families of quail driven from their niche when the land for my house was cleared.

Without warning, I am overcome by grief. When I die—a not-altogether distant prospect now that I am in my 70s—what will become of the creatures who rely on this little piece of earth for their survival? I have come to know and love them as individuals, not just "the deer," "the raccoons," "the coyotes," or "the birds." If nothing is done to prevent it, too many houses will eventually crowd into this space, another small piece of wilderness groomed to death.

My tears open me to a stunning new idea: Even though I cannot restore the ozone layer or reverse the present trend of global warming single-handedly, I can manifest The Rhino's healing power in my own individual way. I can remove myself, my son, my granddaughter, and future generations from the present cultural vortex of acquisitiveness and domination over the natural world, a trend that will eventually destroy the planet if it is not interrupted. I can bequeath my land to the animals. Measured against the emotional rewards of sanctuary for the winged and four-legged folks that I love, profiting from the sale of a desirable piece of land means nothing. The earth's survival may depend on small personal sacrifices. We cannot wait for governments or agencies to set the process in motion.

A few days after this revelation, an e-mail from Pat Britt asks if I know anyone who would enjoy housing the bronze statue of The Rhino for a few months. Now that she is 75, not even The Rhino can protect her from the effects of growing old, so she and Gwen are building a one-story house to accommodate some probable incapacities. The small rental house where they will live in the meantime does not have room for the outward and visible sign of The Rhino. Of course I want him, and I invite him to live in an entryway where everyone who comes to my house or office can see him. Apparently he likes it there, for on the night he moves in, Pat dreams for the second time that he is dancing with a tambourine.

That week the movie *Duma* is showing at the Rose Theatre in Port Townsend. Based on a non-fiction children's book,[90] *Duma* tells of the twelve-year-old boy Xan's perilous journey through the Kalahari desert—also the setting for many of van der Post's stories—to return his pet cheetah to its home in the wild. *Duma* is a myth for our time, emerging into consciousness at a moment when the desire for our species to survive compels us to make common cause with the many forms of life that we have heretofore abused and exploited nearly to the point of extinction. The reckless heroic journey of a young boy is an apt metaphor for what is now asked of us. We must return the cheetahs, rhinos, and polar bears, and our own bodies, souls, and emotions to their instinctive place in the scheme of things, in spite of our civilized lives among concrete, steel, psychotropics, and big bucks.

Warner Brothers denied *Duma* wide national release because it was not expected to be a commercial success, but it managed to find its way to Port Townsend anyway. A trailer for *An Inconvenient Truth*, Al Gore's documentary about the already devastating effects of global warming, was shown along with it. Slightly more than a year later, *The 11th Hour* drove the point home.

I often hear dreams in which the dreamer is instructed to return some wild creature—a bird or animal, a whale or even a small fish—to its natural setting. The personal meaning of such dreams is usually quite clear because they are wont to come to golden-retriever people whose natural spirit has been all but extinguished by the constraints of polite society and political correctness. These are the individuals who must sacrifice an overdeveloped desire to be nice, to be safe, to fit in, to look good, and embark on a quest to free the natural, often irrational, instinctive, part of the psyche that holds the key to healing.

Dreams of this sort always leave me with questions: Do they belong to the dreamer alone or are they also "big dreams" like the ones that native people believe speak to the whole tribe? On the larger "tribal" level, is their meaning literal or symbolic? Similarly, I have to ask whether The Rhino emerged from the depths "only" to heal Pat's body or also as part of a larger project of the psyche to heal the earth, including, of course, saving outer-world rhinoceroses from extinction.

I have walked with variants of this question for more than thirty years. During the early 1970s, Marie-Louise von Franz, an eminent analyst who had been a student and close associate of Jung's, came to Los Angeles to lecture. In a meeting with a group of analysts and trainees—her tribe—she recounted a vision Jung told her eight days before his death in 1961, in which he saw the planet almost completely devastated; however, he said, thank God, a small area of green remained.

The minds of everyone in the room went straight to the specter that haunted us all during the years of the Cold War between the United States and the Soviet Union: a nuclear Armageddon. Today's nuclear threat pales by comparison. In the Twenty-First Century, Jung's vision brings to mind the devastation wrought by mankind's narcissistic domination of the natural world.

Ever the skeptic, though, when von Franz told her story I could not help wondering if Jung's vision depicted his own dying body, for in the language of symbolism, body and earth are one. Her answer to my question was an emphatic *no*, but in spite of her great authority and wisdom, something of equal authority within me—call it the voice of The Rhino—was not convinced. I held the puzzle in my heart and have brought it out and turned it over many times in the ensuing years. There is no doubt that Jung's visionary gifts were formidable. For instance, before the outbreak of the First World War, he saw Europe overrun with dead bodies and oceans and rivers of blood. However, that, too, occurred during a period of extreme personal suffering after his close relationship with Freud was shattered.

I have come to understand that personal and transpersonal views of a dream or vision are not mutually exclusive. On the contrary, they usually go together, for personal suffering is often what opens the door to spiritual, visionary, or healing gifts. It is as if the wound itself creates the eyes to see, the ears to hear, and even the mouth with which to communicate the psyche's larger intelligence.

In practice, it is essential to know the difference between the inner realm of symbols and the literal world outside, between what happens in a dream or fantasy and the same event in ordinary reality. When the spirit descends into matter the two domains get mixed together. Then they have to be separated. In the process we learn that what we fantasize and what we do are not the same thing and do not have the same effects. We learn to observe, understand, interact with, and believe in the complete reality of the inner world, but not to confuse it with the world outside. The inability to distinguish between them is psychosis.

There comes a time, however, when the small personal life joins up with a larger stream and then inner and outer flow together as one. In van der Post's words, there is a "mysterious interdependence of world within and world without,"[91] revealing that at bottom, they are two faces of the same reality. Thus, when a dream or vision is understood deeply enough, its inner and outer meanings do not conflict. They are both true and lead in the same direction. Jung calls this level of reality the *psychoid*. The alchemists speak of it as the *unus mundus*—the unitary world—and it marks the final stage of transformation.

So it is that when Pat Britt put The Rhino at the center of her life and gave him her full attention, her body and soul were healed; while at the same time, his message, like Jung's last vision, pointed to our endangered natural world long before global warming was a detectible reality. As Pat says, speaking for The Rhino, "We must turn away from our arrogance and learn again to live with the rhinos, the crocodiles, and all the natural, instinctive forms of life—now, before they are gone, leaving us alone, alienated, and doomed to extinction."

In the depths of every one of us lives an ancient, savage, rhinoceros-like creature that is both killer and healer. Which side will predominate in the individual life depends entirely on how we relate to it. If we dismiss it, become possessed by it, or try to destroy it in one of the myriad ways at our disposal, it will surely annihilate us, for it is vastly more powerful than our little egos. In its unconscious, untamed form, this part of the human psyche has already made the planet sick; but if we turn to it and listen to its barely intelligible voice, it can help to heal the earth. It cares nothing for our self-indulgent idealisms, rationalisms, nationalisms, and little for the laws of science. It takes us to the abysmal depths of human capability and then it makes us larger.

Today is the time of The Rhino. He offers his roomy, ancient skin for us to grow into. Do it. It is urgent.

# USAGE NOTE

In the bibliography and endnotes:

*CW* refers to a volume of *The Collected Works of C. G. Jung*, edited by H. Read, M. Fordham and G. Adler, translated from the German by R. F. C. Hull, and published in London by Routledge & Kegan Paul, 1953–1978, in New York by Pantheon Books, 1953–1960, and the Bollingen Foundation, 1961–1967, and in Princeton, New Jersey, 1967–1978.

*MDR* refers to Jung's autobiography *Memories, Dreams, Reflections*, recorded and edited by Aniela Jaffé. NY: Random House, 1961.

Biblical references are to *The Jerusalem Bible: Reader's Edition*. Garden City, NY: Doubleday, 1971.

Etymological information is from *The American Heritage Dictionary of the English Language*, with Indo-European roots. W. Morris (Ed.) Boston: Houghton Mifflin, 1981.

# BIBLIOGRAPHY

Acocella, J. "The empty couch: what is lost when psychiatry turns to drugs?" *The New Yorker*, May 8, 2000.

American Psychological Association. "Research reveals clues to who suffers panic attacks. *Monitor on Psychology*, December, 1996.

––––––. "Psychotherapy *is* cost-effective." *Monitor on Psychology*, January, 2000.

AOL News. "Britain warns against giving antidepressants to kids." December 11, 2003.

Bernstein, J. *Living in the Borderland: The Evolution of Consciousness and the Challenges of Healing Trauma*. London and NY: Routledge, 2005.

Dallett, J. O. *The Not-Yet-Transformed God: Depth Psychology and the Individual Religious Experience*. York Beach, ME: Nicolas-Hays, 1998.

DeLillo, D. *Underworld*. NY: Scribner, 1997.

*Discover*. March, 2006.

Edinger, E. F. *Ego and Archetype*. NY: Pelican Books, 1973.

––––––. *Anatomy of the Psyche: Alchemical Symbolism in Psychotherapy*. La Salle, Illinois: Open Court, 1985.

––––––. *Encounter with the Self: A Jungian Commentary on William Blake's Illustrations of the Book of Job*. Toronto: Inner City, 1986.

––––––. *Archetype of the Apocalypse*. Chicago and La Salle: Open Court, 1999.

———. *The Mysterium Lectures.* Toronto: Inner City, 1995.

Eliot, T. S. "Little Gidding." Ellman, R. and O'Clair, R. (Eds.) *The Norton Anthology of Modern Poetry.* NY: W. W. Norton, 1973, pp. 472–478.

Feshbach, S. and Singer, R. D. *Television and Aggression.* San Francisco: Jossey-Bass, 1971.

Freund, J. E. *Statistics: A First Course.* Third Edition. Englewood Cliffs, NJ: Prentice-Hall, 1981.

Gladwell, M. "The tipping point," *The New Yorker,* June 3, 1996.

Glazer, A. "The tunnel ahead." *Fantasy and Science Fiction.* November, 1961, pp. 239–247.

Greenberg, G. "The serotonin surprise." *Discover,* July, 2001.

Griffith, H. W. *Complete Guide to Prescription and NonPrescription Drugs.* NY: The Berkley Publishing Group, 1997.

Groopman, J. "The pediatric gap." *The New Yorker,* January 10, 2005.

Guggenbuhl, A. *The Incredible Fascination of Violence.* Woodstock, CT: Spring Publications, 1993.

Hannah, B. "Some remarks on active imagination." *Spring Magazine,* 1953.

Hopcraft, X. and Hopcraft, C.C. *How it was With Dooms: A True Story from Africa.* NY: Aladdin Picture Books, 2000.

Huxley, A. *Brave New World.* Second Edition. NY: Harper & Row, 1946.

Jung, C. G. *Symbols of Transformation. CW* 5, 1956.

———. *Two Essays on Analytical Psychology. CW* 7, 1953.

———. "Spirit and life." *The Structure and Dynamics of the Psyche. CW* 8, 1960, pp. 319–337.

———. "The phenomenology of the spirit in fairy-tales." *The Archetypes and the Collective Unconscious. CW* 9-I, 1959, pp. 207–254.

―――. *Aion. CW* 9-II, 1959.

―――. "The Swiss line in the European spectrum." *Civilization in Transition. CW* 10, 1964, pp. 479–488.

―――. "Answer to Job." *Psychology and Religion. CW* 11, 1958, pp. 355–470.

―――. *Psychology and Alchemy. CW* 12, 1953.

―――. "Commentary on 'The secret of the golden flower.'" *Alchemical Studies. CW* 13, 1967, pp. 1–56.

―――. "The spirit Mercurius." *Alchemical Studies. CW* 13, 1967, pp. 191–250.

―――. *Mysterium Coniunctionis. CW* 14, 1963.

―――. "The aims of psychotherapy." *The Practice of Psychotherapy. CW* 16, 1954, pp. 36–52.

―――. *Memories, Dreams, Reflections.* A. Jaffe (Ed.) NY: Pantheon, 1961.

―――. Letter to Oskar Schmitz written May 26, 1923. *Psychological Perspectives,* spring, 1975.

―――. *The Visions Seminars.* Zurich: Spring Publications, 1976.

―――. "Diagnosing the dictators." *C. G. Jung Speaking.* W. McGuire and R. F. C. Hull (Eds.) Princeton: Princeton University Press, 1977, pp. 115–135.

―――. "The Houston films." *C. G. Jung Speaking.* W. McGuire and R. F. C. Hull (Eds.) Princeton: Princeton University Press, 1977, pp. 276–352.

―――. *Nietzsche's Zarathustra: Seminar Notes.* J. L. Jarrett(Ed.) Princeton: Princeton University Press, 1988.

Luhrman, T. M. *Of Two Minds: The Growing Disorder in American Psychiatry.* NY: Knopf, 2000.

Meier, C. A. *Ancient Incubation and Modern Psychotherapy*. Evanston: Northwestern University Press, 1967.

National Public Radio. *All Things Considered*. November 6, 1990; February 22, 2000.

*Seattle Times.* January 21, 2000.

Smith, M. C. *A Social History of the Minor Tranquilizers: the Quest for Small Comfort in the Age of Anxiety*. NY: Pharmaceutical Products Press, 1985.

*Time.* May 31, 1999; August 16, 1999; January 10, 2003.

Trow, G. W. S. *The New Yorker*. March 31, 1997.

Turco, R. *Closely Watched Shadows*. Wilsonville, OR: Book Partners, 1998.

*U.S. News and World Report*. "Violent children and the clues they leave." June 1, 1998, p. 18.

van der Post, L. *A Story Like the Wind*. NY: Harcourt Brace, 1972.

————. "Appointment with a rhinoceros." *A Testament to the Wilderness*. Zurich and Santa Monica: Daimon Verlag and The Lapis Press, 1985, pp. 111–134.

von Franz, M.-L. "The problem of evil in fairy tales." *Evil*. The Curatorium of the C. G. Jung Institute, Zurich (Eds.) Evanston: Northwestern University Press, 1967, pp. 83–119.

————. "On active imagination." *Methods of Treatment in Analytical Psychology*. I. F. Baker (Ed.) Fellbach: Verlag Adolf Benz, 1980, pp. 88–99.

# NOTES

FRONT MATTER

1. "Appointment with a Rhinoceros." *A Testament to the Wilderness*, Zurich and Santa Monica: Daimon Verlag and The Lapis Press, 1985, p. 128.
2. Letter to Oskar Schmitz written May 26, 1923. *Psychological Perspectives*, spring, 1975, p. 81.


CHAPTER 1. FREEING THE SPIRIT TRAPPED IN SICKNESS

3. *CW* 14, p. xiii.
4. *CW* 8, par. 602.
5. *CW* 9-1, par. 388.
6. For example, January 10, 2003.
7. *A Story Like the Wind*. NY:Harcourt Brace, 1972.
8. *CW* 14, par. 293.
9. *Ego and Archetype*, p. 257.


CHAPTER 2. THE RHINO

10. Written with Pat Britt and The Rhino.
11. "The problem of evil in fairy tales." *Evil*, The Curatorium of the C. G. Jung Institute, Zurich (Eds.) Evanston: Northwestern University Press, 1967, p. 102.
12. *CW* 5, par. 492.
13. *CW* 12, par. 547.
14. *CW* 12, par. 24.
15. *CW* 14, par. 206.

16. *Ancient Incubation and Modern Psychotherapy*, Monica Curtis (trans.). Evanston:Northwestern University Press, 1967, p. 53.
17. *CW* 12, par. 26.
18. *CW* 12, par. 29.


CHAPTER 3. HOW TO LISTEN TO THE RHINO

19. *Encounter with the Self: A Jungian Commentary on William Blake's Illustrations of the Book of Job.* Toronto: Inner City, 1986, p. 9.
20. *CW* 14, par. 706.
21. Edinger, E. F. *Anatomy of the Psyche.* La Salle: Open Court, 1999, pp. 5–6.
22. *CW* 14, par. 749.
23. *CW* 14, par. 706.
24. "Some remarks on active imagination." *Spring Magazine*, 1953, p. 38.
25. MDR, p. 189.
26. "On active imagination," *Methods of Treatment in Analytical Psychology*, I.F. Baker (Ed.). Fellbach: Verlag Adolf Benz, 1980, pp 88–99.
27. Jung, C. G. *The Visions Seminars.* Zurich: Spring Publications, 1976, Vol. 2, p. 498.
28. *CW* 13, par. 20.
29. *MDR*, p. 174.
30. *CW* 16, par. 98.
31. Edinger, E. F. *Archetype of the Apocalypse.* Chicago and La Salle: Open Court, 1999, p. 35.
32. *CW* 7, pars. 343–344.
33. "Some remarks an active imagination," *loc. cit.*
34. *MDR*, pp. 185–187.
35. *loc. cit.*
36. "Diagnosing the dictators," *C. G. Jung Speaking: Interviews and Encounters.* Wm. McGuire and R.F.C. Hull, Eds. Princeton: Princeton University Press, 1977, pp. 115–135.
37. *CW* 14, par. 623.

CHAPTER 4. TERESA

38. *CW* 8, par. 646.
39. Paraphrased by Jung in CW 13, par. 239. Brackets mine. I also discussed this story in *The Not-Yet-Transformed God*, York Beach, ME: Nicolas-Hays, 1998, pp. 5ff.
40. *CW* 10, par. 918.
41. *The Mysterium Lectures.* Toronto: Inner City, 1995, p. 63.
42. *Little Gidding.*


CHAPTER 5. THE PARADOXICAL GOD OF VIOLENCE

43. *CW* 11, par 746.
44. *C. G. Jung Speaking. loc. cit.*, p. 303.
45. *CW* 9-II, par 142.
46. *Ibid.*, par 141.
47. *Archetype of the Apocalypse. loc. cit.*
48. Revelation 16.
49. Gladwell, M. "The Tipping Point," *The New Yorker*, June 3, 1996; Turco, R. *Closely Watched Shadows.* Wilsonville, Oregon: Book Partners, Inc., 1998, p. 62.
50. *The American Heritage Dictionary.*
51. *CW* 14, par. 206. Emphasis mine.
52. *The Incredible Fascination of Violence.* Woodstock, Connecticut: Spring Publications, 1993.
53. *Ibid.*, pp.146–147.
54. *Time*, August 16, 1999.
55. *Discover*, March, 2006.
56. *All Things Considered.* National Public Radio, Nov. 6, 1990.
57. *Nietzsche's Zarathustra, Seminar Notes*, James L. Jarrett (Ed.). Princeton: Princeton University Press, 1988. 2 volumes, p. 884.
58. See above, pp. 69–70.
59. New York: Scribner, 1997.
60. *Ibid.*, p. 810.

61. *U.S. News and World Report*, "Violent children and the clues they leave," June 1, 1998.
62. Feshbach, S., and R. D. Singer. *Television and Aggression*. San Francisco: Jossey-Bass, 1971.
63. *Time*, May 31, 1999.
64. *Seattle Times*, January 21, 2000.

CHAPTER 6. SEDATING THE SAVAGE

65. *Brave New World*. NY: Harper & Row, second edition, 1946, p. 92.
66. *Ibid.*, p. xix.
67. *Ibid.*, p. xvi.
68. *Ibid.*, pp. 263–64
69. This and the following historical information is taken from Smith, Mickey C. *A Social History of the Minor Tranquilizers: the Quest for Small Comfort in the Age of Anxiety*. NY: Pharmaceutical Products Press, Inc., 1985.
70. *Fantasy and Science Fiction*. November, 1961, pp. 239–247.
71. *All Things Considered*. National Public Radio, February 22, 2000.
72. *The New Yorker*, March 31, 1997.
73. *Time*, May 31, 1999.
74. "Psychotherapy *is* cost-effective." *Monitor on Psychology*, American Psychological Association, January, 2000.
75. Acocella, Joan. "The empty couch: what is lost when psychiatry turns to drugs?" *The New Yorker*, May 8, 2000.
76. *Of Two Minds: The Growing Disorder in American Psychiatry*. NY: Knopf, 2000.
77. *Time*, May 31, 1999.
78. Freund, John E. *Statistics: A First Course*. Englewood Cliffs, NJ: Prentice-Hall, Third Edition, 1981, p. 367.
79. This information is taken from two sources:
    a. Griffith, H. W. *Complete Guide to Prescription and NonPrescription Drugs*. NY: The Berkley Publishing Group, 1997 Edition.
    b. Acocella, *loc. cit.*

80. This information is taken from three sources:
   a. Greenberg, G., "The serotonin surprise." *Discover*, July, 2001.
   b. Groopman, J., "The pediatric gap." *The New Yorker*, January 10, 2005.
   c. AOL News, "Britain warns against giving antidepressants to kids," December 11, 2003.
81. "Research reveals clues to who suffers panic attacks," *Monitor on Psychology*. American Psychological Association, December, 1996, p. 23.
82. *CW* 10, par. 175.
83. *loc. cit.*, p. 288.
84. Letter to Oskar Schmitz written May 26, 1923. *loc. cit.*, p. 81.
85. *loc. cit.*, p. 211.


CHAPTER 7. THE END AND THE BEGINNING

86. Quoted by Laurens van der Post, "Appointment with a rhinoceros." *A Testament to the Wilderness*, *loc. cit.*, p. 129.
87. *Ibid.* The friend who gave me the book knew nothing about The Rhino nor that I was working on this book.
88. *Living in the Borderland: The Evolution of Consciousness and the Challenges of Healing Trauma.* London and New York: Routledge, 2005, p. 9.
89. As I write this the doe appears outside my window followed closely by her newborn twin fawns. A few days earlier, another doe gave birth just a few feet from the crowds, carnival rides, noise and lights of the annual Rhododendron Festival.
90. Hopcraft, X., and Hopcraft, C. C., *How it was With Dooms: A True Story from Africa*. N.Y.: Aladdin Picture Books, 2000.
91. *loc. cit.*, p. 129.

# Books from *Pleasure Boat Studio: A Literary Press*

(Note: Caravel Books is a new mystery imprint of Pleasure Boat Studio: A Literary Press. Aequitas Books is another imprint which includes non-fiction with philosophical and sociological themes. Empty Bowl Press is a Division of Pleasure Boat Studio.)

*The Shadow in the Water* • Inger Frimansson, trans. fm. Swedish by Laura Wideburg • $18 • **a caravel mystery**
*The Woman Who Wrote "King Lear," And Other Stories* • Louis Phillips • $16
*Working the Woods, Working the Sea* • Eds. Finn Wilcox and Jerry Gorsline • $22 • **an empty bowl book**
*Weinstock Among the Dying* • Michael Blumenthal • fiction • $18
*The War Journal of Lila Ann Smith* • Irving Warner • historical fiction • $18
*Dream of the Dragon Pool: A Daoist Quest* • Albert A. Dalia • fantasy • $18
*Good Night, My Darling* • Inger Frimansson, trans. fm. Swedish by Laura Wideburg • $16 • **a caravel mystery**
*Falling Awake: An American Woman Gets a Grip on the Whole Changing World—One Essay at a Time* • Mary Lou Sanelli • $15 • non-fiction • **an aequitas book**
*Way Out There: Lyrical Essays* • Michael Daley • $16 • **an aequitas book**
*The Case of Emily V.* • Keith Oatley • $18 • **a caravel mystery**
*Monique* • Luisa Coehlo, trans. fm. Portuguese by Maria do Carmo de Vasconcelos and Dolores DeLuise • fiction • $14
*The Blossoms Are Ghosts at the Wedding* • Tom Jay • essays and poems • $15 • **an empty bowl book**
*Against Romance* • Michael Blumenthal • poetry • $14
*Speak to the Mountain: The Tommie Waites Story* • Dr. Bessie Blake • 278 pages • biography • $18 / $26 • **an aequitas book**
*Artrage* • Everett Aison • fiction • $15
*Days We Would Rather Know* • Michael Blumenthal • poetry • $14
*Puget Sound: 15 Stories* • C. C. Long • fiction • $14
*Homicide My Own* • Anne Argula • fiction (mystery) • $16
*Craving Water* • Mary Lou Sanelli • poetry • $15
*When the Tiger Weeps* • Mike O'Connor • poetry and prose • 15
*Wagner, Descending: The Wrath of the Salmon Queen* • Irving Warner • fiction • $16
*Concentricity* • Sheila E. Murphy • poetry • $13.95
*Schilling, from a study in lost time* • Terrell Guillory • fiction • $17
*Rumours: A Memoir of a British POW in WWII* • Chas Mayhead • nonfiction • $16
*The Immigrant's Table* • Mary Lou Sanelli • poetry and recipes • $14
*The Enduring Vision of Norman Mailer* • Dr. Barry H. Leeds • criticism • $18
*Women in the Garden* • Mary Lou Sanelli • poetry • $14
*Pronoun Music* • Richard Cohen • short stories • $16
*If You Were With Me Everything Would Be All Right* • Ken Harvey • short stories • $16
*The 8th Day of the Week* • Al Kessler • fiction • $16
*Another Life, and Other Stories* • Edwin Weihe short stories • $16
*Saying the Necessary* • Edward Harkness • poetry • $14
*Nature Lovers* • Charles Potts • poetry • $10
*In Memory of Hawks, & Other Stories from Alaska* • Irving Warner • fiction • $15
*The Politics of My Heart* • William Slaughter • poetry • $13
*The Rape Poems* • Frances Driscoll • poetry • $13
*When History Enters the House: Essays from Central Europe* • Michael Blumenthal • nonfiction • $15
*Setting Out: The Education of Lili* • Tung Nien • trans. fm Chinese by Mike O'Connor • fiction • $15

## Our Chapbook Series:

No. 1: *The Handful of Seeds: Three and a Half Essays* • Andrew Schelling • $7 • nonfiction

No. 2: *Original Sin* • Michael Daley • $8 • poetry

No. 3: *Too Small to Hold You* • Kate Reavey • $8 • poetry

No. 4: *The Light on Our Faces: A Therapy Dialogue* • Lee Miriam Whitman Raymond • $8 • poetry

No. 5: *Eye* • William Bridges • $8 • poetry

No. 6: *Selected New Poems of Rainer Maria Rilke* • trans. fm German by Alice Derry • $10 • poetry

No. 7: *Through High Still Air: A Season at Sourdough Mountain* • Tim McNulty • $9 • poetry and prose

No. 8: *Sight Progress* • Zhang Er, trans. fm Chinese by Rachel Levitsky • $9 • prosepoems

No. 9: *The Perfect Hour* • Blas Falconer • $9 • poetry

No. 10: *Fervor* • Zaedryn Meade • $10 • poetry


## From other publishers (in limited editions):

*Desire* • Jody Aliesan • $14 • poetry (an empty bowl book)

*Deams of the Hand* • Susan Goldwitz • $14 • poetry (an empty bowl book)

*Lineage* • Mary Lou Sanelli • $14 • poetry (an empty bowl book)

*The Basin: Poems from a Chinese Province* • Mike O'Connor • $10 / $20 • poetry (paper/ hardbound) (an empty bowl book)

*The Straits* • Michael Daley • $10 • poetry (an empty bowl book)

*In Our Hearts and Minds: The Northwest and Central America* • Ed. Michael Daley • $12 • poetry and prose (an empty bowl book)

*The Rainshadow* • Mike O'Connor • $16 • poetry (an empty bowl book)

*Untold Stories* • William Slaughter • $10 / $20 • poetry (paper / hardbound) (an empty bowl book)

*In Blue Mountain Dusk* • Tim McNulty • $12.95 • poetry (a Broken Moon book)

*China Basin* • Clemens Starck • $13.95 • poetry (a Story Line Press book)

*Journeyman's Wages* • Clemens Starck • $10.95 • poetry (a Story Line Press book)


## Orders:

Pleasure Boat Studio books are available by order from your bookstore, directly from PBS, or through the following:

**SPD** (Small Press Distribution) Tel. 800-869-7553, Fax 510-524-0852
**Partners/West** Tel. 425-227-8486, Fax 425-204-2448
**Baker & Taylor** Tel. 800-775-1100, Fax 800-775-7480
**Ingram** Tel. 615-793-5000, Fax 615-287-5429
**Amazon.com** or **Barnesandnoble.com**

Pleasure Boat Studio: A Literary Press
201 West 89th Street
New York, NY 10024
Tel / Fax: 888-810-5308
*www.pleasureboatstudio.com / pleasboat@nyc.rr.com*

Printed in the United States
118206LV00001B/277-309/P